MW01016560

GLOBAL DEMOGRAPHICS

Fund Raising for a New World

Judith E. Nichols, Ph.D. CFRE

Bonus Books, Inc., Chicago

99 98 97 96 95 5 4 3 2 1

Library of Congress Cataloging-in Publication Data

Nichols, Judith E.
Global demographics : fund raising for a new world / Judith E. Nichols.
p. cm.
Includes bibliographical references and index.
ISBN 1-56625-047-1 (cloth)
1. Fund raising. 2. Population psychology. I. Title.
HV41.2.N529 1995
361.7'068'1—dc20 95-34025

Bonus Books, Inc.
160 East Illinois Street
Chicago, Illinois 60611

Printed in the United States of America

Contents

Introduction

I wrote my first book, *Changing Demographics: Fund Raising for the 1990s*, hoping to alert my American development colleagues to the dramatic changes that were taking place in the U.S. population. Many have told me that the ideas set forth in *Changing Demographics* and my subsequent books have encouraged them to reevaluate their methods of fund raising in response to the shifting paradigms.

Over the years, increasingly, I have heard from fund raisers in Canada, Europe, and the United Kingdom that they, too, need and want this information. Many have used *Changing Demographics* but asked for a book "without the American emphasis." *Global Demographics: Fund Raising for a New World* is that book.

Written especially to introduce all fund raisers to the basics of audience segmentation, *Global Demographics* concentrates on providing information on:

who our current donors are
and
who our best prospects might be

Expanded and updated, *Global Demographics* has been organized to be useful for all fund raisers. It has been written especially for those with little or no experience in targeting donors and prospects. A lively "read," *Global Demographics* provides the basics in an entertaining format. You'll recognize your donors and prospects as well as your friends, family, and self.

I have been truly fortunate to be able to call upon the expertise of numerous colleagues as I gathered information for this book. While the list is too long to include everyone I would like to acknowledge, I must offer a very special thank you to those with whom I work closely at the

International Fund Raising Workshop and the Institute of Charity Fund Managers: Per Stenbeck, Ken Burnett, Giles Pegram and Stephen Lee. I also want to extend my sincere appreciation to George Smith, who first invited me to speak at the International Fund Raising Workshop and piqued my curiosity as to similarities and differences in population trends around the world.

Judith E. Nichols, Ph.D., CFRE

PART I

Understanding the New Paradigms

Our prospects and donors of the future are already ordained: only those who have already been born—or are most likely to be born—can be counted upon to fund the missions of our charities and not-for-profits.

Harold (Bud) Hodgkinson, a noted demographer, asserts that "demography is destiny." Hodgkinson says that today's four-year-olds will do one simple but important thing: They will grow up to become tomorrow's adults. That is a demographic certainty.

Hodgkinson offers four underlying demographic truths that he says shape who's who in our populations:

1. With medical advances, better nutrition, and healthier lifestyles, people are living longer. **Our populations are aging.**

2. The more people that are born in the same year as you, the harder you must compete for resources and recognition.

This truth has shaped the lives of mid-life **Baby Boomers**, the largest generational grouping ever seen in the developed world.

3. The number of children born to single people and those over the age of 65 tends to be low. The commitment of **women in the workforce** to new life patterns has redefined households and lifestyles, leading demographers to call it "the single most significant societal trend of the twentieth century."

4. Some people have more children than others and thus will be overrepresented in future populations. Because immigrants, generally, are younger and have a cultural disposition towards larger families, the populations of the developed nations are **diversifying.**

I would add one more "truth":

5. Different generations have different points of reference. Today, more people are alive who were born after World War II than those who were born before it. For young adult **Busters** and youthful **Boomlets** it's a whole new world.

> **These five major societal trends—overall aging and increasing longevity, the unique demographics and psychographics of mid-life Boomers, new life patterns due to women in the workforce, the diversification of our populations, and the different perspective of the young—will significantly affect who you will raise money from and how you will need to approach these prospects and donors.**

Part One of *Global Demographics* "sets the stage" for exploring these truths in depth, providing a quick overview of the formal jargon of demographics and psychographics, and giving thumbnail sketches of our changing world and its equally changing populations.

1 A Quick Lesson on Demographics and Psychographics

To effectively build an expanded and upgraded donor base, fund raisers need to use targeted marketing—combining geographic, demographic, and psychographic consumer attributes—to impact consumer behavior.

Let's start with some basic definitions:

Demographics gives you an understanding of larger-scale similarities and trends.

- **Demographics** are sets of characteristics about people that relate to their behavior as consumers. This, of course, is what our donors are. Age, sex, race, marital status, education, and income are used most frequently. Because fund raisers rarely raise all their funds from a single person, we look for demographic similarities so we can mass market to groups of individuals.

- **Geodemographics** integrates population and geographic

characteristics, specifically relating to a particular population and its location, such as a neighborhood, into demographics.

■ **Segmentation** divides a large population into smaller groups with like characteristics. To make demographic and geodemographic information useful for markets, we segment it.

Elements of Consumer Segmentation and Targeting

- Geographic
  - Regional cultural/economic
  - Census geography
  - Non-census geography
- Demographic
  - Age, sex, race
  - Education, occupation, income
  - Household characteristics
  - Residence
  - Life stage
- Psychographic
  - Social values and beliefs
  - Attitudes, interests, opinions
  - Lifestyles
  - Benefits

SOURCE: American Demographics Institute.

Once we know who, demographically, our target individuals or groups are, we need to understand what makes one individual or group act the same as or differently from another.

Psychographics, according to Arnold Mitchell, who originated the psychographic approach to market segmentation, describes "the entire constellation of a person's attitudes, beliefs, opinions, hopes, fears, prejudices, needs, desires, and aspirations that, taken together, govern how one behaves," and that in turn, "finds holistic expression in a lifestyle."

Psychographics provide the human dimension to understanding consumers and prospects. It is based on the recognition that two individuals may be very much alike demographically, yet act very differently.

■ **Psychographics** are the measure of attitudes, values, or lifestyles. Taken from surveys and observations, they can be integrated with demographic measure to put "flesh" on an individual or group of persons.

There may be, for example, two upscale baby boomers, one of whom is wholeheartedly acquisitive while the other purposely disdains whatever is in vogue. The psychographic approach identifies these people's needs, concerns, self-image, and personal style. Responding to the clues that signal how an individual views him- or herself can enable the knowledgeable fund raiser to do a better job of cultivation and solicitation.

In conclusion: Fund raisers need to **target markets**—using the full range of elements of consumer segmentation and targeting (consumer attitudes) to most effectively impact on consumer behavior. With this basic understanding of what demographics and psychographics are, you are ready to explore how changing demographics and psychographics can be used by your organization.

2 What We've Learned about Our Changing World

To effectively raise money, you must understand how the world is changing.

Change presents both opportunities and challenges. While it can be threatening, disruptive and anxiety-provoking, change is also transforming, revitalizing, and a source of energy.

Unfortunately, too often, change takes us unaware. Then, we play "catch up": trying desperately to move to the new reality. David Parradine, the recently-retired CEO of the United Way of Oregon, USA, notes that "Change is not negotiable. It's inevitable." In fact, the Chinese proverb and curse—"May you live in interesting times"—is especially appropriate given the tumultuous changes that are happening all around us. The one thing we know for certain about the future is that it's likely to be different from the present.

Simon George, Director of Development at the Good Shepherd Trust, Great Britain, suggests trying this test to check your response to change. Does your organization:

- predict change and move ahead of it?

- recognize things have changed and manage to catch up?
- not even notice that change has occurred?

Notes Simon, "No prizes for guessing which will survive to meet tomorrow's needs!"

Let's introduce a term: paradigms. We live our lives based on paradigms. Paradigms are the assumptions that help establish boundaries. They provide us with:

- rules for success
- a filter for incoming experiences and data so that we can accept what fits and ignore the rest

Paradigms are both common and useful. **However, when you develop a terminal case of certainty you wind up with "paradigm paralysis."**

A Paradigm "Example"

Look at a deck of cards. What color are hearts? Spades? We expect them to be red and black, respectively. Why? No reason except that's the paradigm.

(In fact, an experiment reversed the colors—making hearts black and spades red. It took the majority of those asked to review the deck three passes to discover what was different.)

To thrive, not just survive, you need to understand the changing paradigms in population, values, and technology. Becoming fixated on the paradigm you're comfortable with is dangerous!

Futurist Joel Barker notes, **when the paradigm shifts, everyone goes back to zero.** Your past successes no longer count . . . they guarantee you nothing! In fact, your successful past can block your vision of the future.

You can't plan for the future if you're evaluating from the past and present. Unfortunately, there is a natural resistance to change. To overcome this resistance, you need to have solid, useful information to evaluate.

What are the changing demographic paradigms that fund raisers must understand to succeed in the years ahead? The changing paradigms fall into two general areas:

Aging Around the World

	United States
Current 65+ population	28.5 million or 12% of population
Projected by 2020	51.4 million or 17.3% of population
Life expectancy	78 years for women; 71 years for men
	Canada
Current 65+ population	2.6 million or almost 12% of population
Projected by 2021	5.8 million or 16% of population
Life expectancy	79 years for women; 73 years for men
	United Kingdom
Current 65+ population	8.7 million or 15.3% of population
Projected by 2025	11.3 million or 19% of population
Life expectancy	77 years for women; 71.3 years for men
	Germany
Current 65+ population	13 million or 21% of population
Projected by 2020	16 million or 30% of population
Life expectancy	77 years for women; 70 years for men
	Sweden
Current 65+ population	1.5 million or 16% of population
Projected by 2020	1.8 million or 19.2% of population
Life expectancy	80 years for women; 74 years for men
	Japan
Current 65+ population	13.88 million or 11.3% of population
Projected by 2025	31.5 million or 24% of population
Life expectancy	World's longest: 81.4 years for women; 75.6 years for men
	Belgium
Current 65+ population	1.6 million or 15.8% of population
Projected by 2020	2.2 million or 21.5% of population
Life expectancy	79.6 years for women; 73.7 years for men

increasing longevity
and
increasing diversity

INCREASING LONGEVITY: In case you haven't noticed, the world is turning gray. According to demographer Peter Laslett, "Europe and the West are growing old and will never be young again."

The results of gains in medicine, education and nutrition, and declining birth rates are contributing to increasing longevity, the dramatic increase of older persons throughout the world. There are more of us living longer than ever before.

Increasing Longevity

- Lengthening of life
- Middle-aging Boomers
- Female Elders

Another major reason: the aging of the large group of persons born in the years directly after World War II—the Baby Boomers. Twice as large in numbers as the preceding generation, they can only get older, not younger. Currently in their 30s and 40s, as boomers move through life, they substantially increase whatever age group they occupy.

The proportion of the population aged over 50 has increased dramatically. In 1951, only 28% of the United Kingdom's population were "greys": in 1994, this figure stands at 31.3% (about 18 million individuals). By the year 2024 it will have risen to 40.2% (about 23.5 million). By then, some observers claim, nearly half of all British adults will be aged 50 or over.

And increasingly, because women live an average of seven years longer than men, the oldest in our populations—those responsible for the final disposition of estates—will be female.

INCREASING DIVERSITY: No longer will our best prospects be similar to one another. We will deal with diversity between age groups, lifestyles, and ethnic/racial backgrounds.

As life lengthens out, there will be more differences among age groups. Our "generational anchors" will not be the same. We have different points of reference and different childhood experiences.

Increasing Diversity

- Distinct Generational Differences
- Growing Ethnic/Racial Pluralism
- Differences in Lifestages and Lifestyles

Throughout the developed world, more adults are alive who were born after World War II than before it: Seventy percent of adults don't remember "before tv."

Different life experiences mean that fund raisers and prospects may lack common life "triggers." Our philanthropic personalities and our attitudes toward money will not be the same. Fund raisers will need to do more "intergenerational" selling.

In addition to differences between the age groups, we will need to add in differences in lifestyles and lifestages. A growing number of adults are moving through life at their own pace: postponing or not having children, taking sabbaticals from careers, returning to school, starting new businesses, etc. Remarriage, second families, and caregiving change the way adults of similar ages look at their ability to be charitable.

Try targeting MOBY's (Mommy Older, Baby Younger) and DOBY's (their daddies). Once Yuppies (Young Urban Professionals), now they're PUPPIES (Poor Urban Professionals) and WOOF's (Well-Off Older Folks).

We've got Sandwichers (adults caught between caring for their children and their older parents); SKIPPIE's (School Kids with Income and Purchasing Power) as well as groups based on special interests like Global Kids (children with strong feelings about the environment plus strong influence over family purchase choices); and New Health Age Adults (consumers who consider their health and the health of the planet top priorities).

Fund raisers will also be dealing with an increasingly culturally and ethnically diverse base of prospects. Nonprofits need to learn how to be inclusive with client populations, volunteers, trustees, and donors.

How Can Fund Raisers Use This Information?

The increasing longevity and diversity of our populations will change the way we do fund raising in fundamental ways. Too many fund raisers are still working under the old rules: assuming an unlimited pool of donors to be acquired, treating everyone as if they share common "generational anchors," and clinging to methodologies that today's savvy consumers are rejecting.

> ***Remember: "when the paradigm shifts, everyone goes back to zero." No matter how successful you have been, you must change your methodologies or lose ground.***

Your Options for Dealing with Change:

- Ignore it and chance death
- Study trends and adjust to them
- Anticipate events and move first
- Lead and make things happen

SOURCE: *The Marketing Mystic*, Edward S. McKay. Revised by Arthur M. Rittenburg, Amacom 1994.

Here are the fundamental changes*:

Because people are living longer:

- Concentrate on renewal and upgrading donors rather than acquisition of new prospects
- Concentrate on planned giving rather than current sacrificial (major) giving
- Differentiate between donors by generational triggers

---

*This chapter provides a brief overview. An in-depth explanation of each of the points discussed is provided in Chapter 11.

Because the majority of adults were born after World War II:

- Use US $100 (UK £75) as a meaningful benchmark for giving
- Accept that there is less donor loyalty

Let's briefly look at each paradigm shift, in turn.

Because people are living longer:

■ Concentrate on renewal and upgrading donors rather than acquisition of new prospects:

Research has shown that it takes five times as much work to attract a new customer (donor) as to renew and upgrade an existing one. Because of their increasing longevity, the donor you attract at age 40 can continue to give, year after year, for 30, 40, 50 or more years.

■ Concentrate on planned giving rather than current sacrificial (major) giving:

It takes about 15 years for our perceptions to catch up with reality. Right now, most adults do not understand their own increasing longevity. But soon they will. And with this understanding, their willingness to part with assets during their lifetime will decrease.

■ Differentiate between donors by generational triggers:

Different life experiences mean that fund raisers and prospects may lack common life "triggers." Our philanthropic personalities and our attitudes towards money will not be the same. Fund raisers will need to do more "intergenerational" selling.

Persons in their 50s and older tend to be cash payers, distrusting newer technologies. They tend to listen to society's recommendations and like to support traditional, well-established charities. Younger persons are likely to look for more "personal" charities and to dislike workplace giving. They are more participatory in personality style; supporting only the organizations they actively work with. They grew up budgeting for purchases and use newer technologies.

Because the majority of adults were born after World War II:

- Use US $100 (UK £75) as a meaningful benchmark for giving:

Inflation has changed our perceptions of what it takes to make a difference. While Pre- and World War II generations tend to believe that US $25 (UK £10) is a meaningful gift, Boomers and younger adults believe it takes significantly more to accomplish the same goals. As there are more adults who were born after World War II than before, make sure your message fits the larger audience.

- Accept that there is less donor loyalty:

Having grown up in a world where they were always in competition for resources and recognition, middle-aged and younger adults tend to be less forgiving of poor service, mistakes on the part of the organization, and being taken for granted. There is no second chance with Boomer and Buster donors and prospects. You must constantly recultivate.

For the rest of this decade, knowledgeable fund raisers should view our traditional donors—the current Mature Market—as one "in transition." You must position yourself to continue working with this audience—it's the one we've dealt with for the past 30 years. But, simultaneously, you must begin to attract the adults born after World War II (Boomers and Busters) so as to build for the future.

By studying the demographic and psychographic information available on our changing populations, you will be able to increase your opportunities for fund-raising success.

3 An Overview of Changing Populations

Fund raisers deal with individuals of all ages, either directly as prospects or because they influence those who give.

Rebecca Piirto in *Beyond Mind Games: The Marketing Power of Psychographics* describes a study by DuPont and Management Horizons that focused on shared experiences. It uses as a starting point the assumption that people are shaped by the events they experience during youth. "People of the same age tend to behave in similar ways because they went through the same formative experiences. During the formative years—between the ages of 7 and 21—core values and attitudes are shaped that will affect an individual for life."

As people mature, other influences take over, such as college, marriage, pursuing a career, and/or raising a family. Overriding all of these personal influences are the broader events—political, social, international, technological and economic—that shape all of our lives.

As a result, we have different points of reference and different childhood experiences.

Each generation has its own personality.* To understand the differences between generations, we need to ask how they were raised as children, what public events they witnessed in adolescence, and what social mission elders gave them as they came of age.

Projecting the cycle is a new way of predicting consumer attitudes and lifestyles. There are four "generational personalities"—idealistic, reactive, civic, and adaptive—which recur in that order throughout history. To succeed in reaching the generations, your messages will have to pay attention not only to where a generation has been but also to where it is headed. (The terms "cohort" and "generation," though often used interchangeably, are not exactly the same. A generation is usually defined by its years of birth. Cohorts are better defined by events that occur at various critical points in the group's lifetime.)

Currently, we are dealing with seven generational groupings or cohorts, spanning from pre-1901 to those born today. I've combined the oldest groupings together because the numbers are extremely small, and concluded that there are five age groups we must understand.

As the developed world moves deeper into the 1990s and nears a new century, our prime audiences will be:

CIVICS: Our oldest cohort grouping, now aged 70 and older, have "civic" personalities—believing it is the role of the citizen to fit into society and make it better. Civics are today's activist elderly.

Civics came of age during the Depression and many of them fought in World War I and II. Their shared experiences gave them two key characteristics: frugality and patriotism. They are the 20th century's confident, rational problem-solvers, the ones who have always known how to get big things done.

---

* Historians William Strauss and Neil Howe in their book, *Generations: The History of America's Future, 1584 to 2069*, suggest that we can read behavior along a "generational diagonal." Their ideas are relevant not only for U.S. fund raisers but throughout the developed world. The Henley Centre in London has adapted this work for the United Kingdom and Europe.

To make this information useful for fund raisers, I have sifted through a number of demographic and psychographic theories concerning cohorts, incorporating other theories into the main one proposed by Howe and Strauss and the Henley Centre.

Generations in the 20th Century

Birth Years	Generation	Lifestyle	Financial Style
1903 - 1922 European 1900 - 1924 USA	DEPRESSION or G.I.	CIVIC “We fought for it”	CAUTIOUS “Save, save, save”
1923 - 1939 European 1925 - 1945 USA	SILENTS	ADAPTIVE “We earned it”	BALANCED “Save, then spend”
1940 - 1957 European 1946 - 1964 USA	BABY BOOM	IDEALISTIC “We deserve it”	GREEDY “Spend, then save”
1958 - 1974 European 1965 - 1977 USA	BABY BUST	REACTIVE “We won’t get it”	RESIGNED “It’s hopeless”
1975 - 1994 All	BABY BOOMLET	CIVIC	PROTECTED

Civics have boundless civic optimism and a sense of public entitlement. Former boy and girl scouts, they volunteer and give because it is part of their inner image. They respect authority, leadership, civic-mindedness and discipline.

- **Preferred message style:** rational and constructive, with an undertone of optimism.

> "We're quicker to laugh, and not as eager to blame. There's time left in this game.
>
> "May we find (along with the inability to tell ourselves that we'll keep playing forever) a few compensations."
>
> —Judith Viorst, *Forever Fifty*

- **Financial style:** Shaped by memories of the American stock market crash and the Great Depression, Depression Babies have cautious spending habits. Always mindful of the lessons of their childhood, their money personalities are conservative. They tend to be cash payers and distrust the technology of the "cashless" society.

- **Key life events:** The Depression and World War I and II

THE SILENT GENERATION: born in the years leading up to and during World War II, this smaller group of "young elders" was taught to be "silent," believing in the will of the group rather than individuality. War Babies growing up during "the war to end all wars" learned to be "seen but not heard." Followers rather than leaders, they will respond to appeals to their other-directed pluralism, trust in expertise, emulation of the young, and unquenched thirst for adventure.

Consensus builders rather than leaders, they make the best of things. Silents give freely to charity, are inclined to see both sides of every issue, and believe in fair process more than final results. They are organization-loyal and value-oriented.

- **Preferred message style:** sensitive and personal, with an appeal to technical detail.

- **Financial style:** Their parents drilled the lessons of the Great Depression into them but Silents reached adulthood in golden economic days, benefitting from real estate appreciation, a booming stock market, portable pensions, government entitlements, and inflation. Now in or approaching retirement, many World War II Babies appear willing to spend on themselves if not on charity. Their financial style is "save a little, spend a little."
- **Key life events:** World War II, the dropping of the bomb on Hiroshima, and the Cold War as symbolized by the Berlin Wall.

BABY BOOMERS: Our societies' adult "idealists" (born during the optimistic years following World War II) have been hard for the world to swallow. Boomers were told they could do anything. Life is a voyage of self-discovery. They display a bent toward inner absorption, perfectionism, and individual self-esteem. Taught from birth that they were special, boomers believe in changing the world, not changing to fit it.

"I plan to do the 'someday' things." —Robert Goodnow, the 42-year-old who became the mayor of Old Saybrook, Connecticut, in 1989.

"The '90s will be like the '50s but less conventional." —Sally Jackson, PR consultant, defining the aging Baby Boomer style as "New Fogey."

- **Preferred message style:** meditative and principled, with an undertone of pessimism.

Notes Barbara Caplan, vice president at Yankelovich Clancy Shulman, a marketing research firm, "They have a higher level of optimism, a sense that the world is their oyster."

In midlife, Boomers will see virtue in austerity and a well-ordered inner life. Also, they will demand a new assertion of community values over individual wants.

"This will be a much more open and challenging and possibly skeptical set of people," says Rena Bartos, marketer, on the aging of Baby Boomers.

- **Financial style:** Having always lived in a world of inflation and having no memories of the Depression, they have a different understanding of money. This is the generation who saw money lose clout. More is worth less. Financial planning is viewed as a sign of status in its own right. However, they are coming out of the free-spending 1980s to focus on non-materialistic values. They tend to buy first, pay later, and they like monthly payment plans and using credit cards.
- **Key life events:** the assassinations of John and Robert Kennedy and Martin Luther King Jr.; world-wide rock music (the Beatles), the swinging sixties, the IRA, the Red Brigade, and other youth-based terrorism.

BABY BUSTERS: the "reactive" young adults born to early Boomers are the first generation that doesn't believe life will be better for them than their parents. Following the much-heralded boom, the media convinced us that busters could do nothing right.

They were the throwaway children of divorce and poverty, the latchkey kids. Reactives weren't trusted or appreciated as youth and carry the scars into adulthood. They are the most conservative-leaning youths of the 20th century. Busters will need convincing proof that your organization is reliable and will simplify rather than complicate their lives.

"My generation considers the baby boomers too self-absorbed and frivolous. While our parents—the "Happy Days" generation—were pampered children of the 1950s, my generation grew up with childhood memories of waiting in long gasoline lines. The first of us came of political age during the Iranian hostage crisis. And while the nation appeared prosperous during the Reagan years, many of us now know that our generation was left with the bill for a decade of budget deficits and an enormous savings-and-loan bailout," says Taegan Goodard, 26, in an interview in New York *Newsday*.

- **Preferred message style:** blunt and kinetic, with an appeal to brash survivalism. "I want us to be the generation that leads, that votes, that earns, that spends, that doesn't continue to let our parents fight our wars for us," notes Nicholas W. Nyhan, graduating senior, in a commencement speech at the University of Massachusetts in Amherst, Massachusetts, USA. They see their role in life pragmatically. They want to fix rather than change. They are highly influenced by technology and television.

- **Financial style:** Twentysomethings have a different view of the good life. Only 21% say the most important measure of living the good life is financial success, and a scant 4% believe that the criterion is owning a home. The rest are more concerned with the acquisition of intangibles: a rich family or spiritual life, a rewarding job, the chance to help others, and the opportunity for leisure and travel or for intellectual and creative enrichment.

Still being supported in adulthood by parents, many have high discretionary income they will give to charities they work with. Highly computer literate, they prefer the cashless society.

- **Key life events:** The crumbling of the Berlin Wall, opening of Eastern Europe, Band Aid, and Live Aid.

BABY BOOMLET: the "civic" children born to Boomers who postponed childbearing, hold many of the values of an earlier generation. While it may be too early to tell what events in their lives will be significant, it is likely that technology and globalism will play important roles. They are growing up in a world without boundaries and are likely to extend their philanthropy well past their own countries.

GENERATIONAL GAPS IN VALUES

	World War II Generation	Baby Boom Generation	Baby Bust Generation
Personal	Allegiance	Self-discovery	Self-oriented
Political	Conservative	Liberal	Pseudo-conservative
Social	Law & order	Altruistic, humanistic	Competitive
Ethical	Fundamental	Moralistic	Situational
Financial	Save & pay later	Buy now, pay later	Almost hopeless
Buying	Based on necessity	Have it now	Whoever has the most, wins
Products	Tools, homes, cars, home appliances	Clothes, entertainment, travel	High-tech gadgets for work and fun
Reward	"I earned it"	"You owe me"	"I want it, but may not be able to get it"

SOURCE: adapted from *Twentysomething: Managing and Motivating Today's New Workforce*, Lawrence J. Bradford and Claire Raines with Jo Leda Martin, Master Media Ltd. 1992.

PART II

Building Your Donor Base

To succeed in the years ahead, you will need to produce a holistic development program—one that respects the identity of each prospective donor segment while recognizing its contribution to a profitable whole. That means we need to look at both the short and long term.

Short-term, not-for-profit organizations need to do a better job of soliciting the current pool of donors and realistic prospects. Martha Farnsworth Riche, the head of the U.S. Census Bureau, has suggested that in the years ahead it is necessary to shift our marketing emphasis from "exploring new markets to exploiting existing ones." The existing markets include:

- Mature Individuals
- Mid-life Boomers
- Women
- Changing households

For long-term development charities need to begin to cultivate the donors of the future. Because of donor attrition, if we don't do this now, eventually our organizations will cease to exist. The newer markets for fund raising include:

- Young adult Busters
- Youthful Boomlets
- Diversified populations

Part two provides you with in-depth information on each of these population segments.

4 Mature Audiences

The "age wave" is coming. Not only are people living longer, but the sheer size of the now middle-aged Baby Boom population plus the lowering of birth rates guarantees that older individuals will increasingly be the focus of fund raisers in developed countries. Ken Dychtwald, writing in his book *Age Wave*, calls this the "most important trend of our time."

The world's elderly population (60 and over) in 1991 numbered nearly half a billion persons. Almost half of those individuals live in just four countries: The People's Republic of China, India, the Soviet Union, and the United States. And, in developed countries, percentages are generally high and increasing: they range from a low of 9% in Japan to 40% in Sweden, with notably high figures in Denmark, Canada, the United Kingdom, Germany, Italy, and France.

Focus on discretionary income, not wealth. Because most older individuals live alone or with just a spouse, per capita discretionary income is high for these households.

GLOBAL AGING

Comparative Indicators and Future Trends

The World's Oldest Countries: 1991

(Percent of population aged 60 and over)

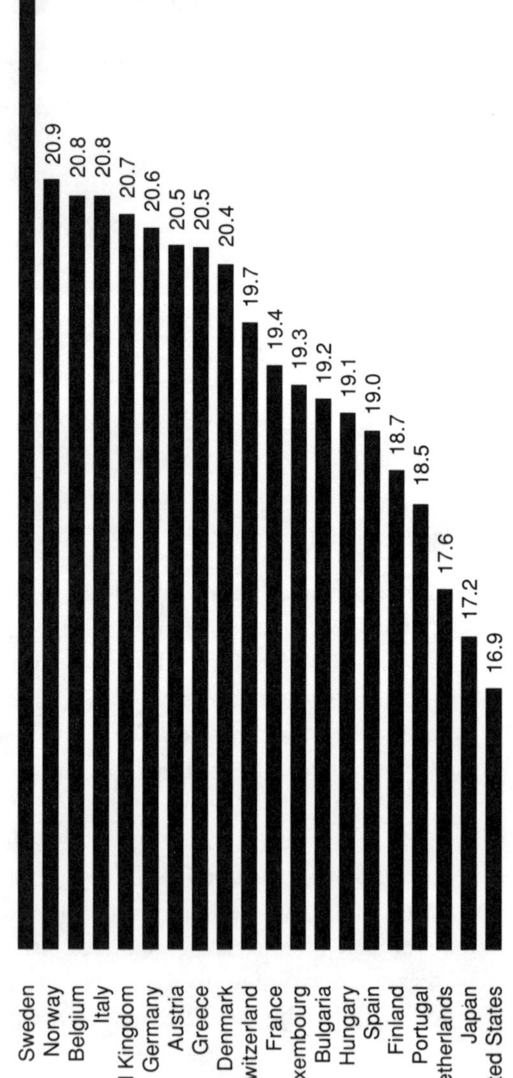

OPALS (Older People Active Lifestyles) are a heterogeneous, individualistic group, worthy of your organization's focus. People over 50 control much of their nations' wealth and do most of the volunteering. Knowing that because of the aging worldwide, this target population is booming—what can your organization do to get an increased share of their contributions?

A Changing Market

Mature households contribute more to charitable causes (12% greater in the United States, for example) than does the average household. In the USA, they contribute more than average to religious organizations, charities, and political candidates, in that order, but less than average to educational institutions.

As the Baby Boomers age, this may change. Tomorrow's older individuals will be better educated and more affluent. They will have fewer relatives, two or more incomes, multiple pensions, better retirement plans, and better health. They will live longer, retire earlier, and be more concerned with the quality of life than is today's mature person. Their interests may be very different from their parents and grandparents and the causes they support may change as well.

Also different will be attitudes toward money. Older individuals still remember when modest dollars had major muscle. Those currently 70 and older were deeply influenced in their youth by the terribly hard and financially frightening times of the 1920s and 1930s. The next generation—World War II Babies—bear some scars but have moderated their financial conservatism because of the increasing personal prosperity (or optimism of its happening) following World War II. For both Depression Babies and World War II Babies, however, annual gift giving is often pegged at US $25 or UK £10. It is usually very difficult to upgrade contributions from these population segments.

However, today's middle-aged adults and tomorrow's older prospects are Baby Boomers. Individuals born in the mid-1940s and later were fully immersed as consumers in the free-spending, affluent decades following World War II, try as their parents (and grandparents) did to inculcate in them a sense of financial practicality. Their point of view about money is somewhat different from that of their parents and is totally at odds with that of their grandparents. For adults now in their mid-40s and younger, you need to ask for contributions at a level that reinforces their sense of what will make a difference—a minimum request of US $100 or UK £75.

For the rest of this decade, knowledgeable fund raisers will view the Older Market as one "in transition" and will work both with the more traditional audience and to build for the future.

Marketing to Affluent Older Individuals

Where are they found? Here is a snapshot of the industrialized countries with significantly increasing older populations: In the United States, the vast majority—88%—of Americans 65 or over live independently and can care for themselves. By 2020, they will comprise 51.4 million or 17.3% of the population, up from 28.5 million, and 12% of the population currently. They are living longer, healthier lives with time for travel, new interests, second careers, education and volunteerism. The over-50 set controls about $7 trillion, or nearly 70% of the net worth of all U.S. households, and are more willing than in the past to spend. They

Aging in the United States: Statistical Snapshot

Current 65+ population	28.5 million or 12% of population
Projected by 2020	51.4 million or 17.3% of population
Life expectancy	78 years for women 71 years for men
Geographic concentration	Southeast, East and West Central
Economic ability	Significant

are geographically concentrated in the Southeast, East Central and West Central states. The most affluent can be found in Connecticut, Florida, Hawaii, Nevada, New Jersey, Arizona, Oregon, and Michigan.

In Canada, the 65-plus population is currently growing at a rate of 3% compared with 1% expansion for the general population. By 2010, with the aging of the baby boom, one in five Canadians will be over 65. Most Canadians over 65 live independently. Their incomes have risen considerably in recent decades, thanks to state pensions indexed to inflation, improved private pensions and high interest rates that have given some retired persons more income than when they worked. Eventually, the 50-plus set will account for half of all discretionary spending power. They tend to be found in small urban centers with populations of less than 30,000.

Aging in Canada:
Statistical Snapshot

Current 65+ population	2.6 million or almost 12% of population
Projected by 2021	5.8 million or 16% of population
Life expectancy	79 years for women 73 years for men
Geographic concentration	Small urban centers with populations less than 30,000
Economic ability	Not yet recognized

In the United Kingdom, the number of seniors is stabilizing, although a spurt is expected after the turn of the century which will increase the projected 65+ population to 11.3 million or 19% by 2025. Ninety-seven percent live in private households, although this drops to 81% among the over-85 set. Unlike the United States and Canada, there is no mandatory retirement nor is there a geographic concentration of older persons.

Aging in the United Kingdom: Statistical Snapshot

Current 65+ population	8.7 million or 15.3% of population
Projected by 2025	11.3 million or 19% of population
Life expectancy	77 years for women 71.3 years for men
Geographic concentration	Nationwide
Economic ability	Not yet recognized

Aging in Germany: Statistical Snapshot

Current 65+ population	13 million or 21% of population
Projected by 2020	16 million or 30% of population
Life expectancy	77 years for women 70 years for men
Geographic concentration	Currently larger cities, shift to rural and suburban areas projected
Economic ability	Moderate, but growing

Germany, according to World Health Organization statistics, is leading the way toward a "senior society" among industrialized nations. In 1982, the median age in Germany was 37, compared to 33 in France, 30 in the United States, and 23 worldwide. By 2020, persons over 60 will make up 16 million or 30% of the population. Currently concentrated in larger cities, retirees have a slightly higher than average income. Within the next 10 to 20 years, as the new cohort moves into the 60-plus group, they should do well financially.

Sweden is expecting a projected 80% increase of people over 80 between 1977 and 2000. Though the overall numbers of older individuals are small, by 2020 they will be over 19% of the population. Concentrated in rural areas, older Swedes enjoy comparatively generous pensions. A survey by the Swedish Bureau of Economics found that since 1975, the real disposable income of retired citizens has increased at a much higher rate than for salaried employees.

Aging in Sweden: Statistical Snapshot

Current 65+ population	1.5 million or 16% of population
Projected by 2020	1.8 million or 19.2% of population
Life expectancy	80 years for women 74 years for men
Geographic concentration	Tends toward rural
Economic ability	Significant

Japan's Ministry of Health and Welfare announced in 1988 that the country had attained world leadership in longevity, surpassing the United States and Europe. By early in the 21st century, Japan will be the most aged country in the world, with one in four citizens over 65. Concentrated in three prefectures, Shimane (15.3% pop.), Kohci (14.5% pop.), and Kagoshima (14.2% pop.), the "Silver Market" (over

60) is growing as an economic force. Marketing research by a leading insurance company estimates the size will grow 6.3 times from 1983 to 2000, from Y23 trillion (approximately US $175 million) in 1983 to Y146 trillion (approximately US $11.1 billion) in the year 2000. The average savings for 60-plus households is Y11.6 million (approximately US $88,000) versus Y7.3 (approximately US $55,000) for households nationwide.

Aging in Japan: Statistical Snapshot

Current 65+ population	13.88 million or 11.3% of population
Projected by 2025	31.5 million or 24% of population
Life expectancy	World's longest at 81.4 years for women 75.6 years for men
Geographic concentration	Top three prefectures: Shimane (15.3%) Kohci (14.5%) Kagoshima (14.2%)
Economic ability	Growing ability

Aging in Belgium:
Statistical Snapshot

Current 65+ population	1.6 million or 15.8% of population
Projected by 2020	2.2 million or 21.5% of population
Life expectancy	79.6 years for women 73.7 years for men

Marketing to Affluent Mature Markets

Five key values determine the likely behavior of older individuals:

- autonomy and self-sufficiency
- social connectedness
- altruism
- personal growth
- personal revitalization

(Personal revitalization includes the need for play, the need for change of pace and change in activities, and the need for rest and relaxation.)

Older individuals are cautious spenders: While the available statistics indicate that many older individuals have significant discretionary income, they are not quick to spend it. They are value-oriented and more willing to try something new if they perceive it as adding value to their lives. Remember, we're talking about people who have experienced more profound social changes in their lifetime than any other cohort.

- Older people are concerned about outliving their assets because of unexpected major expenses (e.g., health care, nursing home).
- Because they retire early and live longer today, older people need to finance a longer post-retirement, often a lifestyle similiar to the one they were accustomed to before retiring.
- Older people have a money personality which has conditioned them to be thrifty and careful with money.

Segmenting the Mature Market

Today's mature market is more properly viewed as having distinct demographic sub-groups, each differing demographically and psychographically. Recognizing that the mature market is not monolithic can help fund raisers to plan marketing strategies that appeal strongly to key older prospects. To successfully tap the rich potential of the mature market, today's fund raiser must look to both the present and the future.

Because people develop the value systems, morals and attitudes that are carried through their lifetime by the time they turn 12, we need to break the mature market into categories: 50 to 64, 65 to 74, and 75 and over. (Some marketers prefer to subdivide the last group into 75 to 84 and over 85.) There are distinctly different patterns with differing emphasis on wants and needs.

Frank Conaway, president of PrimeLife Advertising, notes that "the 'older' population, 50 to 64, generally have grown children and are taking a serious look at retirement. They lead a pre-retirement lifestyle more like that of a 45-year-old rather than that of a 70-year-old."

Because economic conditions differed, we find that the 75-plus group is different than the 50-plus group. The older group remembers trying to raise families during the Depression when they were young. Their children, now in the 50-to-64 group, were able to realize a quality of life and living standards after World War II that far exceeded anything their parents and grandparents ever thought possible.

■ **The "older" population (aged 50 to 64):** Currently, this is the largest segment of the mature market. This group will grow slowly to the year 2000, then grow rapidly as more and more baby boomers join older brothers and sisters.

Men and women in this age group are, in many ways, at the high point in their adult lives. The children are grown, the mortgage is paid, and they have the highest disposable income of any age group. They are better educated and more affluent than their parents were at the same age. This group is extremely direct-mail responsive because of having been conditioned by the massive direct-response industry.

Their lifestyle focus—health, self-fulfillment, a broad spectrum of social activities, comfort, and what to do with their increasing spare time—has prompted some advertisers to refer to the 50-64 year olds as "SUPPIES" (Senior Urban Professionals) or "OPALS" (Older People with Active Lifestyles). As they grow a bit older, they become "RAPPIES" (Retired Affluent Professionals).

Many of these pre-retirement individuals are "possession" experiencers, people whose satisfaction comes from establishing their status. They are purchasers, not ready to give up the opportunity to own more material goods. However, many consider themselves to be "in transition." Not quite sure where retirement will take them, they are often reluctant to make commitments (both financial and for volunteering or attending) to your organization. It's especially important that you not lose contact with these often affluent prospects: be patient until they move to the next psychographic level.

■ **The "elderly" (aged 65 to 74):** are the second-largest mature segment. While this group will hardly increase at all through 2000, it will grow rapidly after that. Though income drops with retirement, spending does too, giving this group a higher disposable income than the "older" population.

Often newly retired, the major source of income for this group is private and government pensions and savings. The "elderly" receives 80% more income than average from estates, trusts, dividends, and rentals. The value of their assets is almost 21% greater than average. At this stage of life, the number of female-headed households begins to climb.

While spending is about the same as for the pre-retired, the emphasis shifts. For many individuals, this is what they hoped retirement would be all about. Decreased costs and/or different priorities have left them with the ability to free up substantial discretionary money for what now matters.

The consumer behavior of older individuals, especially in terms of discretionary spending, is influenced far more by levels of maturity than by a person's age, asserts marketing consultant David Wolfe. While some retirees will remain "possession"-focused, many of our affluent, older prospects will turn heavily toward either "catered" or "being" experiences:

> **"Catered" experiencers:** have developed a greater interest in experiences such as travel, education, or sports. They are willing to pay for intangible experiences as well if you package philanthropy as part of a membership club.
>
> **"Being" experiencers:** have reached an anti-materialistic state when people derive the greatest satisfaction from simple pleasures and human contact. More inner-directed than "catered" experiencers, they are less interested in recognition and formal appreciation. "Being experiencers" are the group we've tended to access for major giving. However, this was based on life spans of 70-75 years. As people recognize they are living into their 90s, will they still be willing to make major gifts in their 60s?

As a sub-group, the "elderly" are the most cynical of our older population. In the United States, for example, they lived through Vietnam, racial riots, and televangelism along with their Boomer children. In the United Kingdom, the IRA's terrorism took its toll on the population's trust. As a result, they require more facts, more information, more cultivation and tend not to be direct-mail responsive.

■ **The "aged" (aged 75 to 84):** is projected to grow quickly through the year 2000, then grow slowly until the year 2032. By the time they reach 80+, two-thirds of the "aged" population will be female.

■ **The "very old" (aged 85 and over):** are the smallest but most rapidly growing segment of mature adults. Households headed by people aged 85 and older receive only half of the average household's income. This group's income from estates, trusts, dividends, and rentals is more than twice the average. The "aged" and the "very old" have assets with a value of 5% above average. The "aged" and the "very old" continue to have faith in our organizations.

Often, communications with charities have taken the place of departed friends and relatives. A wistful comment to *The New York Times* from an 80-year-old woman: "My personal correspondence has dwindled because many of my old correspondents are dead, and my children are busy with their own affairs. The solicitations fill the gap." These individuals are the most direct-mail responsive. They are also our best prospects for legacies and life income gifts.

Working the Marketing Niches

Jeff Ostroff, author of *Successful Marketing to the 50+ Consumer*, suggests that our aging populations have seven promising "niches of need." These needs are (1) the home, (2) health care, (3) leisure time, (4) personal and business counseling, (5) educational services, (6) financial products and services, and (7) products that combat aging. Not-for-profits should market themselves as providing solutions to these needs.

The Evangelical Covenant Church, for example, markets Covenant Retirement Communities, located near several key retirement areas, as combining safe, secure, burden-free independent living with outstanding health care and a multitude of leisure activities. Targeting those 62 and over, its ads in *New Choices*—a publication aimed at affluent, active mature individuals—help the Evangelical Covenant Church to identify persons sympathetic to its objectives. Those who request information—whether or not they decide to retire in a Covenant community—are ideal prospects for planned giving.

Avoiding Negative Myths

The major problem in marketing to older persons is that our cultures are deeply gerontophobic. Ken Dychtwald, author of *AgeWave*, notes that "We have a fear of aging and a prejudice against the old that clouds all our perceptions about what it means to grown old."

Dychtwald lists six prevalent negative myths and stereotypes that blind us:

Myth l: People over 65 are old.
Myth 2: Most older people are in poor health.
Myth 3: Older minds are not as bright as young minds.
Myth 4: Older people are unproductive.
Myth 5: Older people are unattractive and sexless.
Myth 6: All older people are pretty much the same.

The key to reaching older persons is to market positively.

More frequent communications are the key to keeping and upgrading your older prospect. Use longer letters, case examples, testimonials. Provide facts and figures along with a narrative. Be prepared to follow up with phone calls. Remember, a person who begins giving to you in his or her 50s may live to be 90. With renewal and upgrading, you are cultivating a major donor.

> **With all older adults, images and text will more successfully invoke values if they are indirect.** And remember, *the eyes degenerate first.* By age 42, most people can't read eight point type. Check your brochures as well for light against dark and bright against dull to increase visibility.

Use appropriate role models. Mature individuals are attractive. Use photographs that emphasize vitality. Use situations that are active. Robert B. Maxwell, American Association of Retired Persons president, notes that while the young are getting older, "the old are getting younger. The 70-year-old today is more like the person of 50 from 20 years ago. We have not yet found the fountain of youth, but research has shown that healthy older people can enjoy most of their mental and physical abilities and even improve them."

Use appeals which leave autonomy and independence intact. Use the term "older individuals," "mature persons," or "aging" rather than "elderly" or "senior citizens." And say "50 years or over" rather than "or older." Position your planned-giving appeals to discuss financial well-being.

TARGETING MATURE INDIVIDUALS

- ☐ **Avoid age-ism and negative myths**
- ☐ **Segment**
  - ○ **50-64: In transition, pre-retirees**
  - ○ **65-74: Traditional givers, low numbers**
  - ○ **75+: Asset rich, concerns about outliving $$$**
- ☐ **Market positively**
  - ○ **Communicate in length/depth**
  - ○ **Use appropriate age models**
  - ○ **Watch signs, type size, color usage**
- ☐ **Match your organization to their niches of concern 1) home 2) health care 3) leisure 4) education 5) personal & business counselling 6) aging 7) financial products and services**

Retirement does not mean vegetating! Older individuals look forward to new opportunities to learn, work, and be of service. Eckerd College, a small liberal arts school of 1,300 students in St. Petersburg, Florida, began the Academy of Senior Professionals in 1982 to encourage exposing the young to the experience afforded by the older community. The academy has grown to nearly 200 members and associate members. The school benefits as much as the community; many of the participants in the Academy are professionals who have been high achievers and wish to continue being productive. They teach seminars, assist younger students, and form a strong relationship with their adopted college.

Grand Circle Travel, a travel tour company that often works with not-for-profits, targets people aged 50 and older for "extended vacations" of up to 26 weeks. A majority of their customers, says vice president Mark Frevert, are aged 65 and older. More than half are college educated, and their annual incomes exceed $25,000. To attract potential clients, they offer—via direct response coupons—a free brochure called "Going Abroad: 101 tips for mature travelers."

Respect their preferences. Many older persons do not like traveling at night. The Portland Home and Garden Show traditionally opened at 6 pm on a Thursday. In 1988, the opening hour was set at 11 am and attendance went up by 1,500 people on the same Thursday. Older attendees made the difference.

Recognize that life goes on. Even when older persons are not married, many enjoy active relationships. Be careful to include "the significant other" in discussions and invitations. Romance at later ages also brings with it concerns for protecting assets. Sensitive financial planning advice may be welcome by the entire family.

Market using appropriate publications. Some communities have a local seniors paper. Read it regularly and offer to contribute articles on your organization. Ask your advertising agency to review the demographics of the mature market in choosing print, radio and television media.

The older individuals' market will continue to offer fund raisers the greatest immediate potential for both increased contributions and greater volunteer resources. By studying the demographic and psychographic information available on this changing group, you will be able to increase your opportunities for success.

5 Baby Boomers

As we move through the 1990s and into the 21st century, most not-for-profits must target Baby Boomers—that large adult grouping of individuals born following World War II—as new and renewing donors. The reason: the bulk of our population growth will occur because people are living longer rather than because more people are being born. Your contributors tomorrow will be those individuals you attract today!

But, before you design a fund-raising plan targeting Boomers, you need to understand and accept that these prospects—and their giving habits—are dramatically different from the individuals born before World War II.

The Boomer Story

Because of a combination of social, historical and economic factors, child bearing throughout the developed world had been low from about 1915 through the end of World War II. As soldiers began returning home and a mood of optimism set in, demographers predicted confidently that a "boom" would occur. However, no one was prepared for how enthusiastic the boom would be: older women had the children they had postponed and younger women had children earlier. And both groups—reacting to a real or perceived bettering of life—had more children than demographers anticipated.

In every developed nation the Boomer cohort dwarfs the number of older adults and, in most cases, is significantly larger than the numbers of Busters following them. The Boomer impact on our societies, at every stage of their lives, has often been compared to the effects of a very large mouse being eaten by a very small snake: difficult to swallow, hard to digest!

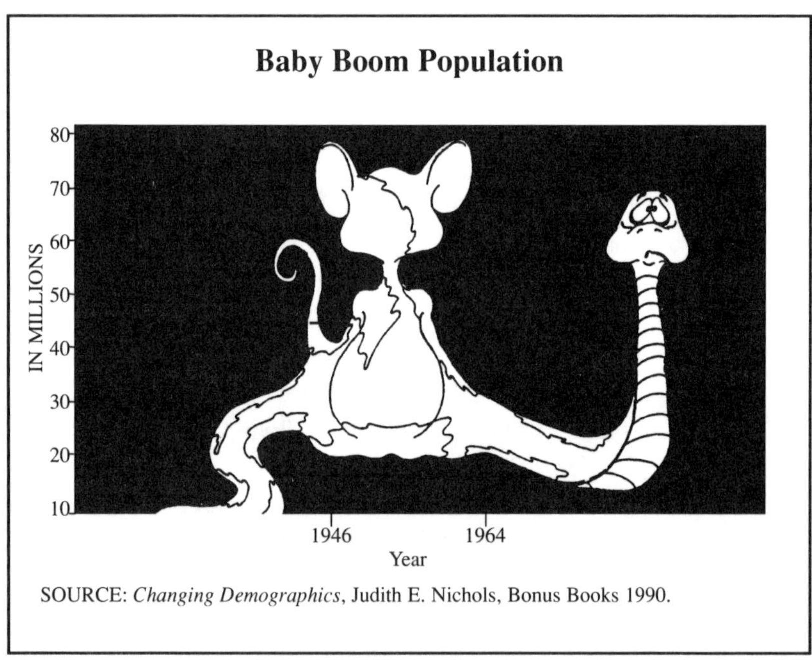

SOURCE: *Changing Demographics*, Judith E. Nichols, Bonus Books 1990.

In the early 1950s, Boomers created growth industries of baby furniture, diaper delivery services, and toy companies. Gerber Foods boasted that "babies are our business—our only business." In the late 1950s, fads like hoola hoops swept the world. In the 1960s, rock music, fast food and snacks, and acne coverups were the rage; then psychedelic fashions, art, and expression took hold. The 1970s? Boomers settling down caused housing costs to skyrocket.

Today, as Boomers swell the ranks of those in their mid-30s through late 40s, they are redefining the idea of middle age. Having elevated fitness to a cult, Baby Boomers are now putting the stamp of approval on plastic surgery. Having discoed their early adult lives away, boomers are staying home more—becoming couch potatoes and cocooning. Having defined a "youth market" for soft drinks and facial cleaning products, Boomers are now the targets for health tonics and revitalizing cremes.

A Generation of Emerging Economic Power

With maturity, Baby Boomers are entering their peak earning years. "The generation is just gaining the economic and political power to shape events," says Bickley Townsend, vice president of The Roper Organization and a contributing editor of *American Demographics* magazine. "The sheer numbers, and their power, mean they will determine which businesses succeed and which fail. Whatever the Baby Boom wants, the Baby Boom is going to get."

Many Boomers feel it's about time. Although Boomers are better educated (twice as likely to have gone to college as their parents), their sheer numbers coupled with a series of rude social and economic shocks (ranging from the social unrest of the late '60s and early '70s to double-digit inflation) have depressed their disposable incomes. Boomers marry later, have children later, and divorce more often. *Time* Magazine, quoting boomer Brian Weiss in the cover story, "Growing Pains at 40," notes that for many Boomers "middle age sounds a bit strange because many of us haven't attained the goals that our parents attained at that age. I mean, how can you be an adult when you don't own a house?"

Landon Y. Jones, whose landmark biography of the baby boom, *Great Expectations*, chronicles the most-recorded generation in history, agrees, but sounds a note of hope:

> Oppressed by its numbers, the boom generation watched its great expectations yield to diminishing expectations as its troubles piled up. By the end of the seventies, *Fortune* Magazine estimated, the Baby Boomers had effectively lost 10 years' income relative to the cohort just ahead of them and

> hardly seemed to have reason to look forward to the future. But that's not the case. In the next decade the baby boom will be moving into its Golden Era. The smoking friction associated with its size will, for once, be minimized. During the 1990s, Baby Boomers will move into their prime earning years, causing the number of affluent households to inflate to unprecedented heights. Increasing numbers of Baby Boomers will turn their education, job experience, marital stability, and investments into a secure income.

Boomers are not like their parents:

Not surprisingly, most people form their core values with regard to how they relate to money during the influential years when they first start working. This makes Boomers significantly different from their parents and grandparents, the donors we have been cultivating and soliciting since the 1960s.

Psychographically, Boomers are both similar to and distinctly different from other generations:

"In many ways, Boomers' primary concerns are the same as their parents and grandparents: home, marriage, family, and work," says Cheryl Russell, former editor-in-chief of *American Demographics* magazine and author of the book, *100 Predictions for the Baby Boom.*

Boomers are:

- married and they believe that marriage is the best way to live
- have one or two children, and many have three
- prefer to spend their free time at home with their families
- have middle-class incomes and are unwilling to take financial risks
- identify themselves as middle-of-the-road or conservative politically
- favor capital punishment
- believe in God and belong to a church

But, notes Russell, "in many ways the baby boom is profoundly different from any generation in history. This means that in the two decades of middle-aged rule that lie ahead, many of the themes important to successful marketing will be new ones. There are four important new themes: globalism, unisex, individualism, and instant gratification." Russell cautions, if you dig a little deeper, you will find that Boomers:

- have gone to college for at least one year and many are college graduates
- are two income couples
- believe men and women should be equally responsible for housecleaning
- own VCRs and microwaves; many have home computers and telephone answering machines
- frequently go to movies, plays, concerts, and museums
- think divorce is acceptable and abortion should be legal

D. Quinn Mills, a professor at the Harvard Business School who teaches courses in human resource management, concurs that "the basic values and aspirations of the baby boom generation differ substantially from those of their parents." In contrast with their parents, Boomers

- are more suspicious of authority (though leadership is accepted by both generations)
- stress fun and enjoyment rather than duty and obligation
- emphasize performance rather than seniority on the job and experience
- focus on opportunity rather than security
- endorse candor rather than tact
- are self-concerned rather than organization-loyal
- stress individuality and differences rather than groups and sameness
- prefer experience to possessions

The trick in marketing to Boomers is combining the traditional and nontraditional in your appeals.

How can we illustrate nontraditional values tempered with traditional values in fund raising? The Live Aid concert is a good example of the mixing of home values and global values. The concert was staged in our living rooms yet it tied audiences to the world. Live Aid raised US $70 million (UK £50 million) in just a few hours.

Boomer Turn-Ons

- Straight talk
- Personal development
- Meeting new people
- Change

Boomer Turn-Offs

- Authority
- Materialism
- Anonymity

As we move through the 1990s and into the 21st century, the graying of the baby boom will redefine aging. Between 1990 and 2000, the age 45 to 54 population segment alone will grow by 45%. Because Boomers are a unique combination of traditional and nontraditional values, it's being suggested that the 1990s will be like the 1950s but less conventional.

"The trick in marketing to the new middle aged is that you will have to bridge the similarities and differences between the baby boom and older generations," concludes Russell. If you pursue only the similarities, you might attract older individuals—those 50 and older—to whatever you're selling, but you won't attract the bulk of Baby Boomers. If you pursue only the differences, you might appeal to the minority of Baby Boomers who are single and childless, but you'll miss most of the boom generation."

Comparing Boomers to Themselves

Using education and income, Peter Kim, senior vice president at the J. Walter Thompson Company—a major advertising firm—has suggested a four-cell demographic segmentation for Boomers:

Yuppies ("Superclass"): high education/high income
Elite Workers: low education/high income
Would-Be's: high education/low income
Workers: low education/low income

For many charities and non-governmental organizations, targeting the Superclass seems obvious, especially for key trustee and volunteer positions and as major legacy and life income gift prospects.* Landon Jones, author of *Great Expectations*, notes that "they are the professional-managerial working couples who command more discretionary income than any other group. They dress differently from most people, entertain themselves differently, eat differently, travel to different places, buy different things, and have different values. They have far fewer children."

But the Superclass is only a small part of the overall Boomer generation (6% with an anticipated growth over time to 11%). You should cultivate Elite Workers as well, who command incomes equal to or better than the Superclass. They comprise approximately 9% of all Boomers.

Would-Be's will then account for 18% of Baby Boomers and Workers for nearly 63%. Should we ignore Would-Be's and Workers? Probably not. While these Boomers—as individuals—may not have the disposable income you may seek, as couples they are often doing very nicely. Remember that, whether in a formal marriage or more informal living arrangement, the majority of Boomer households do contain two full-time working adults.

Quentin Mills suggests a *psychographic segmentation* of Boomers with five key groups:

Contenteds	48%
Pleasure Seekers	25%
Competitors	15%
Trapped	11%
Get Highs	1%

While each lifestyle emphasizes different priorities, life for the majority of Boomers is made up of three interconnected elements: work, personal relationships, and family. And, unlike previous generations, Boomers refuse to have two personalities, one for work and one for their personal lives. They insist on being themselves in both places. They are the first generation to expect work to be fun.

---

*Life income gifts are called planned gifts in the USA. They include insurance, property, appreciated stocks, trusts, and annuities. Planned gifts are discussed in detail in chapter 14.

Smart marketers will also segment early Boomers from later Boomers. Those born in the beginning years of the baby boom differ psychographically from the Boomers who followed in the middle and last years.

Early Boomers found the going rougher than did later Boomers. Often, they were confronted rudely with the reality of the intense competition from their peers. Later Boomers are less idealistic, more realistic, than their earlier cohorts. While early Boomers majored in philosophy and the arts, later Boomers opted for business and engineering.

One late Boomer, Nancy Smith, noted that "it's like, we don't even have a name. Yours—'Baby Boomers'—is so big we fall in its shadow. We're hard to pin down: silent where you were loud, solitary where you were communal, plain where you were colorful."

Boomers share a specific money attitude.

Baby Boomers anticipate higher costs for everything, from cars to contributions. Boomers were fully immersed as consumers in the free-spending, affluent decades following World War II, try as their parents (and grandparents) did to inculcate in them a sense of financial practicality. Their point of view about money is thus somewhat different from that of their parents and is totally at odds with that of their grandparents. Essentially, their attitude is this: "If you have no money in the bank, but have at least two credit cards that aren't over the limit, you're doing fine."

Almost 70% of total income growth between now and the year 2000 will be accounted for by the 35 to 50 age group.

Boomers will account for 40% of the developed world's spending power by the turn of the century. Household income for the 35-50 age group (Boomers of the next decade) will leap 90%. That's in comparison to a 50% growth projected for the public as a whole.

One in three baby boomer households will be affluent by the turn of the century. And, with children leaving the nest, Baby Boomers will increase their discretionary income.

- The only adult groups with an increase in discretionary income will be the 35–54 and the over–65.
- The real aggregate spending power increases over the next five years will come from the 35–54 and the 45–54 households.

What Factors Contribute to Increasing Baby Boomer Affluence?

Baby Boomers are two-earner households. By the end of the decade, the older half of the baby boom will be solidly in its peak earning years. And, much more so than in previous generations, we may be seeing Double Income, Plural Pensions. Dippies can accumulate substantial future retirement resources through plural streams of future retirement income. They can look forward to two government pensions, two occupational pensions and, perhaps, two individual retirement accounts, in addition to their other savings and investments.

As Baby Boomers age, they will accumulate wealth through property ownership, investment, and inheritance.

■ **Older Boomers rode the heady housing market of the 1970s,** often buying first homes at modest rates, then driving up the prices as the demand kept increasing. These older Boomers have substantial assets, though they may not have the cash for current giving. However, their concerns—retirement and educating children—lend themselves to planned gifts. And the older Boomers' psychographics: focusing on the experiences that money can buy should encourage exploration of gifts of property.

■ **Boomers are about to come into their inheritances,** delayed by the increased longevity of their parents and grandparents. In the next 20 years, an unheard of quanity of wealth will pass from a senior generation, famous for making money and babies, to its children the Baby Boomers. Says Alexander Bove Jr., a Boston tax lawyer:

> People are inheriting more and more money every year. My father, a machinist in a shipyard, left a $150,000 estate. In my kids' generation, because of what's happened in terms of parents' real estate appreciation, profit sharing, pensions, and life insurance, we're going to see millionaires created just by the parents dying off. It's nothing now to have half a million dollars' worth of life insurance. If my wife and I dropped dead, my son and daughter will get $1 million *each.*

The majority of Boomers will not inherit until they reach their 50s and 60s. For many Boomers, inherited money will not be used for necessities of life: by that point, they will be comfortable.

Boomer-Driven Niches and Needs

Many are guessing that as Boomers earn more and inherit from previous generations, the money will go to philanthropy. To get a share, you'll have to convince this highly skeptical audience that your charity or non-governmental organization is relevant. There are three key factors to keep in mind when looking for boomer-driven niches and needs:

1. Boomers are an aging population. Currently in or approaching their 40s, Boomers are giving new meaning to "middle age." As the "mouse in the snake," Boomers will redefine every step of their aging.

Demographers William Lazer and Eric H. Shaw note that "in the future, the mature consumer will change. As the baby boom ages, older persons will be better educated and more affluent. They will have fewer relatives, two or more incomes, multiple pensions, better retirement plans, and better health. They will live longer, retire earlier, and be more concerned with the quality of life than today's mature consumer."

Boomers will look, act and feel younger at 50 than previous generations did. "Fifty will be like 40," says gerontologist Fernando Torres-Gil, who predicts that this generation won't confront "old age" until well into their 70s. When the American Board of Family Practice asked a random sample of 1,200 Boomers when middle age begins, 41% said it was when you worry about having enough money for health-care concerns, 42% said it was when your last child moves out and 46% said it was when you don't recognize the names of music groups on the radio anymore!

2. Boomers are a "held-back" cohort. They married later, divorced more often, had children later and, often, have split families. They're fuelling a baby boomlet which will send ripples through those organizations, programs, and services targeted to families and youth.

Cultivate Boomers now for the future. Because Boomers are marrying and having children later—or with divorce, repeating their families—many are still caught in high expenditure years. With the emptying of the nests and their increasing economic stabilization, Boomers will be the audience of the future.

3. Be aware that Boomers are a "sandwiched" generation. Often Boomers—especially Boomer women—are dealing with the concerns and needs of aging parents and grandparents as well as the needs of their growing families.

Are Boomers Philanthropic?

Resoundingly, yes. Raised as "Idealists," Boomers have been taught to put others ahead of themselves. They see themselves as "changing the world," not fitting in with it like their "Civic" and "Adaptive" parents and grandparents.

As the "me generation" has matured, many have moved to a new "ethic of commitment," noted by Daniel Yankelovich in his book, *New Rules*. Tending to be more inner-directed than previous generations, Boomers are committed to a search for self-fulfillment through super-personal relationships and more enduring commitments to the world of work and the business of common survival.

In their 30s and 40s, Boomers are demonstrating a commitment to philanthropy that outpaces that of other age groups. In 1992, more Boomers gave to nonreligious charities than did people in any other age group, according to The Roper Organization, contradicting the view that members of this generation are selfish or unwilling to support causes or institutions financially.

Baby Boomers are willing to give. They know you can't save the world without spending big dollars. Asked properly, these younger, newer donors will gladly give larger dollars than did previous generations. Notes Brian O'Connell, past president of Independent Sector, a U.S. coalition of more than 750 corporate, foundation, and voluntary organizations:

> The dramatic increases in donating time and money among the baby boom generation is good news for today and may suggest even better news for the future as this very large population group assumes community responsibility.

What Will Baby Boomers Support?

Boomers want to make a difference. In the years ahead, quality of life issues—making the world a better place for themselves and their children—will be the main preoccupation of Baby Boomers. Few Boomers believe income dollars alone will improve their styles of living. They know the problems are greater than one individual or one household.

■ "Baby Boomers prefer basic causes related to individual need, like homelessness, over estoreric causes like Boy Scouts, which are seen as doing good but are hard to quantify," says George Wilkinson, senior vice-president for strategic planning at United Way of America. Others say that Boomers are fond of "causes that fell through the cracks" and have been overlooked by mainstream donors, such as domestic violence and gay/lesbian rights.

■ "Baby Boomers want to make things happen with their money," says Ralph Whitehead, a political science professor at the University of Massachusetts. He specializes in Boomer values. "They want to see that a child was fed or that a homeless person got a bed and blanket for the night. To encourage them to give money and get involved you must make the relationship between them and the beneficiary as direct and immediate as possible."

■ "Boomers want to create a sense of community," notes Donna Schuurman, executive director of The Dougy Center in Portland, Oregon and herself a Baby Boomer. "We're looking for new communities, places where we can belong, contribute, and make a dent. We're not as likely to respond to mailings as people used to be. We're more cynical about fund raising, for good reason, and need to be convinced. We want to care and get involved, but aren't always sure how or where. Here's a biggie: we're waiting to be asked."

How Can We Get Boomers to Give?

Donor loyalty is not the Boomer norm: the annual donor organizations counted on year after year for modest but steady giving has all but vanished as Baby Boomers seek out this year's "sexiest" causes. Boomers have more choices in charities than earlier generations (nearly two-thirds of today's not-for-profits were created following World War II) and have shown less allegiance than their parents and grandparents display.

Boomers' early experiences may have conditioned them to disloyalty. For example, although better educated than the general population, Boomers often do not support the colleges and universities they attended. Many believe that the college experience they received was not up to the expectations they had. The overcrowding and lack of individualized attention which was, in truth, a result of so many Boomers crowding into a finite number of colleges and universities has led to a lack of Boomer "brand" loyalty to their achools. When a key life experience lets you down, it may form a pattern you continue when making purchasing decisions.

The heart of the dilemma is that Boomers view themselves as special people. Having been told they were unique from early childhood, Boomers:

- expect organizations seeking their patronage to cultivate them extensively even when they are contributing at modest levels
- prefer to make contributions on a major scale, yet won't or can't commit to the cost up front

To create donor loyalty in Baby Boomers, concentrate on getting ongoing pledges rather than a single, larger gift. The monthly payment is the ultimate involvement device. It helps Boomers buy in to your organization and helps you to identify them for recognition and extra cultivation.

Equally important, monthly payments break the psychological barrier. It enables the Baby Boomer to make a gift at an enhanced level that reflects his/her "apartness from the crowd."

Understand boomer "triggers":

■ **Instant gratification.** Boomers need to "feel" the experience of giving and they want to feel special. It's the result of the competition for resources and recognition they've battled all their lives. Yet few are in a position to make the size gifts that they consider significant. You can help by encouraging them to use standing orders, covenants, direct debits, pledges, and credit card payments to reach larger goals. Remember, most Boomers have grown up on "buy now, pay later."

■ **Recognize all gifts fully.** Don't let too much time go by between receiving and acknowledging a gift. The giving club tiers can become a vital strategy in retaining and upgrading fickle Boomer donors. Plaques, signalling their "in" status, or an invitation to VIP events for "members only" contributes to the boomer's sense of uniqueness and desire for participation.

■ **Increased accountability.** Boomers don't trust anyone. "Nonprofits have to disclose more about their expenditures in a way that can be understood and documented," notes Jack Sims, a minister and head of B.O.O.M.E.R.S. (Believers Outside of Most Every Religious System) Consulting who spends his spare time helping nonprofit organizations better understand the Boomer generation. Sims criticizes one religious broadcaster's pie chart showing half of the organization's income being spent on building new stations and half on "outreach," a word that Boomers find too vague.

■ **"Tell, tell, tell, before you start to sell, sell, sell."** Baby Boomers have been called "information junkies." They want specific information on the issues that interest them. However, they are too sophisticated to respond to intense, emotional appeals. According to John Groman, senior vice president of Epsilon Data Management, "People don't relate to generalities or talk-down-to-them copy. They have to be approached conversationally and told about real programs, case histories, and successes."

■ **Appeals that grab their attention.** The Boomer generation is a stimuli-bombarded generation. As Cheryl Russell notes, the power of instant communication has magnified the boom's size. "Not only does the baby boom have a loud voice, it has a loudspeaker wired into every home." Sims suggests that appeals must be fast-moving, with quick cutaways and facial close-ups to create visual excitement. Use short paragraphs, colorful envelopes, and catchy headlines that can be read quickly at the end of the busy day.

■ **Use their technologies.** Boomers enjoy receiving information but are quick to become impatient with boring formats. Don't be afraid to use newer technologies, including fax machines, VCRs, e-mail, and the Internet, to personalize your message and make it stand out from the messages of other organizations. These technologies are likely to become formidable factors in your fund-raising campaigns. Get comfortable with them.

■ **Provide professional and personal networking opportunities.** Because they are always in competition and time-pressed, Boomers mix work and pleasure. Innovation is the key to attracting their attention. Formulaic black-tie fund raisers are a bore, says one 32-year-old. "You stand around and chat, nibble a canape, sip champagne, adjust your cummerbund, do a slow fox trot, and adjust your cummerbund again." Boomers prefer a more creative party where guests can don anything from jeans to formalwear and dance to louder, faster music.

■ **Use nostalgia.** Marketing themes that focus on nostalgia for the 1950s and early 1960s (music, dress, trivia) are well received. "Nostalgia waxes and wanes, and it's certainly waxing now, as the baby-boom generation passes into phases of life that create conditions that can eleicit nostalgic responses," says Fred Davis, a professor at the University of California at San Diego and the author of *Yearning for Yesterday: A Sociology of Nostalgia*. He and other academics say marriage, parenthood and the leveling off of careers in the late 30s and 40s are typically followed by an unsettled period in people's lives when they look back to childhood for comfort.

Rethink Your Fund-Raising Strategies

■ ANNUAL GIVING: Ask for money at a level that reinforces a boomer's sense of what will make a difference—a minimum request of US $100 or UK £75. Don't confuse what the Boomer wants to do with how he or she can do it: the first is motivation; the second fulfillment.

■ MAJOR GIVING: Redefine your concept of a major donor to acknowledge cumulative as well as annual gifts. Remember, a 40-year-old donor, making an annual gift of $100, will give you $5,000 by the time he or she is 90 years old.

■ PLANNED GIVING: With longer life expectancies, Boomers are unlikely to let go of assets. In the United States, charities suggest the use of single and/or limited premium insurance policies which enable Boomers to make major gifts now. Concentrate on Boomer concerns in marketing life income gifts: the key concerns are retirement, aging parents, and education for children.

Know where to look for affluent Boomers. Unlike their parents, Boomers are less likely to be employees of large corporations. The most successful Boomers tend to be entrepreneurs. Boomers cluster in urban environments rather than rural areas or suburbs.

TARGETING BABY BOOMERS

- ☐ Have been held back 10 years economically
- ☐ Not donor/customer loyal
- ☐ Grew up being told they were special yet overwhelmed by their numbers
- ☐ Don't trust anyone
- ☐ Very nostalgic for "the good old days"
- ☐ Key concerns
  - ○ Retirement
  - ○ Educating their kids
  - ○ Their parents' aging
- ☐ Created networking as a way of life
- ☐ Concentrate on recognition, instant gratification, accountability

6 Baby Busters

While the majority of your time and effort should be spent finding, cultivating, and appealing to mature individuals and middle-aging Baby Boomers, there are also fund-raising opportunities among our younger populations.

Today more persons are alive who were born after World War II rather than before:

- Eighty-five percent are not old enough to remember the 1929 stock market crash.
- Seventy percent don't remember "before TV."
- Sixty-six percent are not old enough to remember before the existence and demolition of Berlin Wall.
- Fifty percent are too young to remember pre-Beatles music.

Who are Baby Busters?

Whenever society has been totally child-focused, eventually it does a flip. That is, in essence, the Buster dilemma. Busters suffer from the natural progression of idealists to reactives. But with a twist: Because of the sheer numbers of Boomers, everything—good and bad—about that generation was exaggerated.

Following the much-heralded boom, Busters could do nothing right. They were the throwaway children of divorce and poverty, the latchkey kids. Busters weren't trusted nor appreciated as youth and carry the scars into adulthood. They are the most right-leaning youths of the 20th century. Unlike Boomers, Busters grew up in relative obscurity under television's supervising eye. Ignored or vilified by the media, they tend to be cautious, anti-intellectual and pessimistic; many are fearful, frustrated, angry and believe they will be exterminated in a nuclear war.

Key Life Events for Baby Busters

The crumbling of the Berlin Wall and opening of Eastern Europe.

In fact, Busters have been given poor media. Today's 18- to 29-year-olds are generally no more—or less—cynical than other age groups. And, especially among college-educated Busters, they are fairly optimistic about their personal prospects.

Comparing aspects of their lives to their parents at the same age finds Busters a mixed bag. Today's 18- to 29-year-olds are one of the most diverse generations in ethnicity, education, and aspirations. They are the results of a culture of choice.

Generally, they are more optimistic than their elders about their personal prospects though they are less optimistic than the baby boom generation was at their age. **The top self-descriptors of Generation X:** fun (88%), outgoing (86%), and sociable (79%). At the bottom of the list are caring (49%), independent (41%), and value-conscious (39%).

They aspire to the traditional values of career, home, and family.

While, on one hand, they are even more accepting of dual-career marriages than Boomers, Busters are also more inclined to plan to have larger families than did the baby boom.

What Busters Want

Every generation is a product of the times in which it comes of age. For many of today's young adults, their economic horizons have been limited. What are Busters like?

- They aspire to a more traditional lifestyle.
- They have turned their attention away from work and towards home, family, and friends.
- They focus on quality rather than quantity of possessions and experiences.
- They are less skeptical than older consumers, more trusting of advertising and the media.

SOURCE: Roper's *The Public Pulse.*

Their preferred message style is blunt and kinetic, with an appeal to brash survivalism. For Busters, "society" doesn't exist. They are worldly with a wide range of experiences.

Their financial style differs as well. Twentysomethings have a different view of the good life. Only 21% say the most important measure is financial success, and a scant 4% believe that the criterion is owning a home. The rest are more concerned with the acquisition of intangibles: a rich family or spiritual life, a rewarding job, the chance to help others, and the opportunity for leisure and travel or for intellectual and creative enrichment.

Young adults are very important to fund raisers:

They significantly influence their parents' philanthropic choices.
They have large amounts of discretionary income of their own.
They are highly philanthropic.

Young individuals have a heavy influence on the philanthropic choices of their families.

- Overlapping the Buster and Boomer generations are increasing numbers of young adults who have returned to live in a parent's home. More than half of never-married persons aged 18 to 24 still live at home. Some 28% of men and women in their 20s now live with their parents. We call these "boomerang kids." Many see themselves as having been forced back home by societal problems and are eloquent about the need for change.

Young people are a growing, though overlooked, market for discretionary spending. Although the economic situation is more pessimistic for Busters than previous generations, many have high discretionary incomes: a combination of their continuing support by parents, postponing marriage and children, and a reordering of personal priorities. This is the "pocket" for charitable giving.

- A growing source of affluence is "leapfrog legacies." Many grandparents are by-passing well-to-do children and leaving money directly to their grandchildren. A recent study by Columbia University found that 25% of all college prepayment plans were being funded by grandparents rather than parents. Also: 14% of private-school tuitions are being paid by grandparents.

- Young adults living at home or at college have their basics paid for by parents. Thirty-nine percent spend more than $50 a week on entertainment—the same money available for charitable giving.

- Perhaps, the most hopeful reason to assume growing affluence among young people is their very moniker: baby bust. Because of its smaller size, (typically one-third to one-half the size of the baby boom) the "bust" will create a new income environment. Sought after by businesses, the competition for qualified Busters will drive up wages and benefits.

Demographers are arguing over whether Busters will have an easier time financially than did the Baby Boomers. There's less cohort competition for jobs, but the baby boom continues to compete for all but entry-level positions. Many do believe that "their demographics are on their side"; the size of the labor pool will drop by the turn of the century.

Baby Busters can afford to be picky with education and jobs. Like Boomers, Busters are postponing marriage. They are staying in school longer and getting their careers underway. The number of young householders is shrinking. By the time the oldest Baby Buster turns 35 at the start of the new century, young householders should be fewer but more affluent than they are today.

And, while their career earnings to date are lower than those of more mature persons, their family responsibilities are fewer and their economic prospects are bright. Larger and larger numbers of younger adults and children will be going on for extended education compared to our adult populations. Notes NYC-based Conference Board chief economist Fabian Linden: "This longer period of financially independent young adulthood amounts to an economic, social, and psychological revolution."

Reaching Baby Busters

Often dubbed "Generation X," the twentysomething crowd are "the New Pragmatists." Growing up with the lessons of 1980s, they have a sense of diminished expectations. Unlike the Boomers, Roper's

The Public Pulse reports that the Busters "grew up in relative obscurity under television's supervising eye."

Notes Lilian Maresch, whose Minneapolis, Minnesota, consulting firm, Generation Insights, tracks generational trends: "The Busters have decided that you can't have it all." The Busters are trying to find stability in an unstable world. As a result they're focused on quality rather than trendiness.

Busters tend to be cautious, conformist, anti-intellectual and pessimistic: many are fearful, frustrated, angry, and believe they will be exterminated in a nuclear war. Research by the Roper Organization reveals Busters to be more conservative than the previous generation. They appear to have little interest in championing causes. However the liberalizing events behind the Iron Curtain have caught their imagination. They don't believe life will be better for them than their parents and see their role in life as pragmatic. They want to fix rather than change.

Busters are decidedly "pro-business" and more than three-quarters of them—compared to 69% of today's Baby Boomers—have favorable opinions of large business corporations. This is even more impressive when you compare that 21% of young adults have a "highly favorable" opinion of large companies, compared to just 12% of the Baby Boomers now and the same number of them in 1978.

And there's a lot of resentment towards the baby boom. Busters think the Boomers took the biggest pieces of the pie and left them with the crumbs. Notes Albert Stridsberg, a New York marketing analyst:

> Their older brothers and sisters, the Boomers kept telling them about the enormous amounts of money they were going to make. But as Busters emerge from college they're finding that there're few or no jobs, that they don't have as wide a choice, and that the glamour industries are jammed with 25- to 35-year-old Baby Boomers. Busters, too, are equipped with MBAs, but they're expected to take the kind of money offered 10 to 15 years ago...They're hostile and suspicious, because they feel cheated.

Philanthropy and spirituality are very important to a majority of teens. The share of teens who agree with the statement, "It's very important to me to get involved in things and help make the world better" increased from 65% in 1989 to 69% in 1992, then fell to 63% in 1993. Those who say their religion or faith is one of the most important parts of their lives increased from 53% in 1989 to 58% in 1992, then fell off in 1993 to 53%.

Busters will give. Busters are the first generation not to equate success strictly in terms of material possessions. "Quality of life" issues will predominate for them—and probably for the boomlet as well.

This has given rise to a whole generation of new charities—more personal in nature than those their parents and grandparents founded. This bodes well for volunteerism and philanthropy. Concerns for AIDS, the environment, and abortion, as well as parenting and positive self-issues, and ongoing education will be "hot."

More practical, less idealistic than Baby Boomers, the 18- to 27-year olds express more confidence in charities and other major institutions, according to a study by the Barna Group. Busters demonstrate a 36% confidence level in nonprofits compared with just 23% for all adults.

Because Busters are pragmatic idealists they will need convincing proof that your organization is reliable and will simplify rather than complicate their lives. They are more participatory in personality style, supporting only the organizations they actively work with.

Research shows Busters are more conservative in their charitable choices than previous generations. They appear to have little interest in championing causes. Unlike the confrontational Boomers, Busters are more likely to negotiate and collaborate than to demonstrate. They enlist the aid of legislators to the causes they espouse. And, having been raised in an era of rapidly expanding communications technology, many are very sophisticated about attracting press attention.

Although Baby Busters are quite philanthropic, they see themselves as having only small amounts of disposable cash to give to charity (their priorities include sharing with a large extended family of friends and colleagues). Their gift fulfillment needs to be structured to allow for a constant stream of extremely modest gift amounts.

Remember that younger persons grew up in a different world. Highly computer literate, they prefer the cashless society: using credit cards, standing orders, direct debits, and electronic transfers. An increased use of electronic newsletters, videos, e-mail and computer bulletin boards should be in your organization's future. Already 1.3 million individuals in the United States, mostly Busters, have used Prodigy for philanthropy. This computer network program allows people to look at information about the economic status of young children, take a brief quiz, and send for information on charities that work with kids.

Marketing to Baby Busters

Your goal in reaching Baby Busters is twofold: to begin their identification with your organization at a modest level of giving and to begin identifying the few who currently can, in fact, make significant gifts.

You need to start by catching their attention. Radio is the best vehicle for reaching Busters. But, unlike Boomers, who seemed to always have rock 'n' roll in common, they don't have a common taste. The Buster "Top 40" embraces everything from rap to reggae to New Age.

(Teen Busters watch more TV than other age groups, but they are also more likely to tune out commericals, says Teen Research Unlimited. Two-thirds change channels during breaks and 89% fast forward through commercials when watching videotaped programs. Which types of of TV spots do teens prefer? Funny or clever ones. Not commercials that rely on celebrities or music. The least-preferred are those with a home-movie style or straight product demonstrations.)

Focus on 18- to 21-year olds. "This is the only group you need to address," says Barrie Webster, president of Berenter, Greenhouse & Webster of New York City. "If you successfully reach this fulcrum group, you ignite the fuse that sets the entire span on fire." Eighteen- to 21-year-olds are admired by teenagers for their independence, says Webster, while young adults admire them for their freedom. Because of this, 18- to 21-year-olds influence lifestyles and product perferences for the whole group, he says.

It's difficult to reach 18- to 21-year olds through most media. They do not read newspapers or magazines often, and they watch an average of only 1.25 hours of television. Webster suggests targeting this middle group on the college campus: 40% are in college. All not-for-profits need to join in the effort to make courses on philanthropy a part of the college curriculum. Consider holding a volunteer fair on campus or at a shopping mall where the community of not-for-profits can work together to demonstrate roles for Busters.

■ *Give them a specific role to play.* Post-Boomers are not trying to change things. They want to fix things. Active projects—planting trees, cleaning up the beaches, painting lower-income houses—are very attractive to them. Keep in mind that teens, probably more than any other consumer group, desire immediate gratification. You may want to tie appreciation tokens to small increments of volunteerism.

■ *Find tie-ins with their studies.* The vast majority of Busters are still in school. The importance of incorporating volunteerism and philanthropy into school cannot be overemphasized. At LaSalle University in Philadelphia, the result is that students have—quite literally—made an investment in the future of the homeless. Members of the Investment Club solicit classmates for donations to what is hoped will become a $50,000 endowment. Revenues, expected to reach $6,000 a year once fully vested, will be contributed to help the homeless in Philadelphia.

■ *Read what they read.* Consider advertising in a college newspaper: about 60% of students report reading four or five of the last five editions. Students are also reached through several out-of-home media vehicles, like wall boards, kiosks and ads placed on campus newspaper stands. Several Buster publications are surfacing: the newest is *Inside Edge* magazine aimed at males aged 15 to 22. Notes editor Aaron Shapiro, "It's written entirely by members of the target market." Shapiro and his partner, Jonathan Hsu, are both 21.

■ *Consider reaching Busters through their Boomer parents.* The largest number of children aged 12 to 17 are found in households headed by 35- to 44-year-olds. Consider holding special events that reach both age groups. For example, Boomer music is surprisingly popular with the Buster generation as well.

■ *Let them go shopping.* It's one of the twentysomethings' favorite leisure activities. Offering merchandise through a catalog that benefits your not-for-profit is a good way to attract a strong list of upscale Busters.

■ *Give them a sense of community.* Even more so than their older brothers and sisters, Busters believe in the importance of friends and family. Consider a named fund that a group can contribute toward for a common goal.

■ *Look for the future entrepreneurs.* A Yale University president gave this advice: "Always be kind to your A and B students. Someday one of them will return to your campus as a good professor. And also be kind to your C students. Someday one of them will return and build you a $2 million science laboratory."

7 Baby Boomlets

Finally, let's meet the younger children of Boomers. At the end of their childbearing cycle, many Boomers have heeded the "biological clock ticking." Because of the size of the boom, it was inevitable that when Boomers decided to have children they would produce an "echo boom" of births.

Known as the "Baby Boomlet," these children repeat the cycle of their grandparents. "Civic" personalities psychographically, Boomlets believe in science and cooperation, and will be easily persuaded that theirs is a good and special group that knows how to build big things together. Society loves them: considering them smarter, better-behaved, and more civic-spirited than the Busters. This is the "smoke-free, drug-free class of 2000."

Boomlets are growing up in a world without boundaries and are likely to extend their philanthropy well past their own country. Their preferred message style: rational and constructive, with an undertone of optimism.

What Matters to the Young?

In a survey of 20,000 students in 45 U.S. cities, fourth-graders gave a clear mandate on their concerns:

- 18% said cleaning up the environment should be the first priority
- The three biggest problems:
  23.6% cite drug use
  17.3% note crime
  16% say it's AIDS

SOURCE: Eastman/Kodak Survey 1993.

Babies are the BMWs of the '90s. Boomlet babies are increasingly being born to dual-career couples who are waiting longer to have children and are thus able to spend more money on them once they arrive. The number of women who are 30 or older when their first child is born has more than quadrupled since 1970; the number of first children born to women over 40 more than doubled between 1984 and 1990.

In affluent families, Boomlets are often the first generation to take comfort for granted. Having grown up being given everything they need and want, Boomlets are often less concerned with their own possessions and anxious to extend "the good life" to other children. Boomlets heavily influence parents and relatives, encouraging families to recycle and reexamine values.

Meet Cassie: A Typical Boomlet

The joy of my life is my daughter, born in 1984. Cassie is a true Boomlet. Since she began walking she took newspapers and cans to the recycling center in her little red wagon. She nags at her brother and father for smoking. She has signed a school pledge not to use drugs. And, at age 7, solemnly informed me she would only have "safe sex"!

Cassie drives much of the family's philanthropy, often encouraging us to see past our own community boundaries to give to causes overseas because they involve other children. During the Christmas season, I can't go past a Salvation Army kettle without providing her with coins. She has her own charity (a shelter for abused women and children) that she supports with her own money.

Both because your younger audiences are the only prospects for the future and because they have such influence on their parents and grandparents, working with them now will have big dividends for your organization in the future.

Households

For many individuals, women in particular, marriage will be only one of many household categories they will experience as adults. The proportion of married persons is declining and never-marrieds represent one of the fastest-growing segments of the adult population. The increase in working women, the graying of our populations, the proliferation of single-parent households, and the increase in minority populations have all given us countless new profiles.

What is a family today? Families have changed, due in large part to the baby boom generation. Family used to mean a father who worked, a mother who stayed home to watch 2.3 kids, and a dog. Today, it can mean a mid-40s, single, minority working mother and her child. Or, a domestic partnership of same or other sex couples. Increasing numbers of families do not contain children. Or, contain adult children who have returned to the nest.

Married life comes in a variety of life-cycle stages.

- **With Children:**

  - Full Nesters—couples with children aged 6 to 17
  - Crowded Nesters—with children aged 18 to 24 at home
  - New Parents—with children only under age 6
  - Young Families—with children both under the age of 6 and aged 6 to 17

This innovative ad targets Boomers who are waiting to have children. It faces a page of coins:

ARE THESE THE ONLY LITTLE ONES YOU WANT AT THE MOMENT?

With no children yet, you could have quite a lot to look after. Quite a lot of money, that is.

And like any responsible guardian, you want only the best for it. At the Halifax we can help make sure you're doing all the right things.

Our expert staff can provide you with free financial planning matched to your individual needs. With advice on pensions or life assurance schemes, for example. Or a rather appealing range of equity based investments. Like unit trusts or PEPs. Making sure your precious savings are as tax efficient as possible.

We'll also provide you with a free annual review. So as your circumstances change, you can be sure your plan's still right for you. Because, who knows, one day you may want some little ones that gurgle. Not clink.

To arrange a chat with one of our financial advisers, simply get in touch with your local Halifax branch.

Or call free on 0800 10 11 10.

FINANCIAL PLANNING FOR YOUNG PEOPLE 

OUR EXPERTISE IS UNDERSTANDABLE.

IS AN APPOINTED REPRESENTATIVE OF STANDARD LIFE, A MEMBER OF LAUTRO, FOR THE PURPOSES OF ADVISING ON AND SELLING LIFE ASSURANCE, PENSIONS AND UNIT TRUST BUSINESS ONLY

Today's little ones are increasingly being born to dual-career couples who are waiting longer to have children and thus able to spend more money on them once they arrive. The baby is a status signal. Unfortunately for fund raisers, that usually translates into less discretionary income to be spent on charities.

The better audiences for giving will be couples without children:

■ Without Children

- Empty Nesters—childless householders aged 50 to 64.
- Honeymooners—householders just under the age of 35.
- Just A Couples—aged 35 to 49.

Honeymooners tend not to be good prospects for giving: they are heavily into investing in possessions. But Empty Nesters and Just A Couples are prime prospects.

Demographers have been tracking a continued decrease in the proportion of households made up of married couples.

■ MALAs—Mid-life Affluents Living Alone.

Again, because of the baby boom, the demographics of who lives alone have changed. While it used to be that we thought of singles in terms of two polarized groups—college-aged kids at one extreme and widowed elderly ladies at the other, by the turn of the century 35- to 54-year-olds will comprise the fastest-growing segment of individuals living alone. And these households—without spouses or children—are more likely to be affluent.

MALAs are not necessarily Yuppies. They're not into conspicuous consumption nor are they compulsive acquisitors. Some points to keep in mind:

- They're not passing through on the way to another stage. Many see being single as a way of life. They are involved in their communities, look to put down roots, and often choose volunteerism as a way to meet people.

- They're home-proud. MALAs have not put buying a home or condominium on hold. They invest in their apartments. As a result, they have an investment in the neighborhood around them and the greater community.

- They're into convenience (these are busy people). And they can afford to pay for it. Catalog shopping, for example, is big. Not-for-profits can tap into this.

- They're into entertainment and leisure activities. Although affluent singles work hard, they also play hard. Whether it's vacations, cultural or sporting events, or hobbies, they are generous to themselves.

■ **The "gay market" is a seriously neglected and very wealthy segment.**

Often, gay consumers have very high income levels, very high educational levels, usually no dependents, and, consequently, very high discretionary income. They're often single, with plenty of disposable income and usually without children.

Affluent gay and lesbian households have very high indices in urban gentrified neighborhoods as well as in the affluent and elite urban areas. There is high incidence in university towns but almost no incidence in rural areas at all.

Gay consumers tend to be trendsetting; they purchase new products ahead of society at large. They are responsive to targeted advertising in their own media, and they have proven to be socially motivated consumers—they vote with their pocketbooks.

Life stage and lifestyle will be increasingly important in determining how much discretionary income is available in a household for charitable giving. Be alert for opportunities as the following life stages change:

- parenting
- grandparenting
- empty nesting
- second family
- elder caregiving
- sabbaticals
- retirement
- second career

9 Women

There are five major reasons for seriously targeting women for your organization's fund-raising efforts:

- Women have increasing economic power.
- Women tend to save more of their incomes than do men. They are more attuned, at an earlier age, to concerns about outliving assets making them prime candidates for planned gifts.
- Women outlive men, controlling the disposition of their own estates and, often, that of the spouse as well.
- Women have a new awareness of the power of the dollars they control. They are choosing charities that reflect their concerns and interests.
- Women are more charitably inclined than men. They make three times the number of donations as do males. Women leave more bequests to charity than do men.

Understanding the Changing Role of Women

Women have new expectations for themselves. The combination of postponed or no marriage, increased education, and a commitment to a career rather than "just a job" has enabled Boomer women to establish independence from their families.

Women's educational levels are rising. Increasing numbers of college and post-graduate students are female. Higher education is clearly associated with better jobs, more continuous careers, and higher earnings.

The average woman today has fewer children than a generation ago. The higher a women's educational attainment, the fewer births she has had, or expects to have. It also is more likely that she plans to have no children. For example some 20% of women with five or more years of college do not plan to have children, compared to only 7% of women who have not completed high school.

The average woman is proud to work. The influx of women in the workforce has been called "the most significant societal change of the 20th century." From statistically insignificant numbers, the percentage of women in the workforce has grown to equal—and in some countries to exceed—that of men.

And, while large numbers of women still work in the "pink collar ghettos" with lower paying salaries, women are beginning to take their place in technologically intensive professions and are moving up the management tiers. Changing attitudes are also propelling women into the ranks of business owners and top company leadership positions. More women are prepared to run companies than ever before, since millions of them have progressed through the ranks in fields that were once male-dominated.

The demographic changes are being accompanied by a resounding change in attitudes. By taking their labor out of the delivery room and into the marketplace women have set in place a dramatic change in our society, the consequences of which will affect everyone—men and women, adults and children.

While nearly all women continue to endorse marriage, they perceive marriage as a responsibility to be shared between both partners through similar roles, with husband and wife working to contribute earned income and with both husband and wife sharing homemaking and child-rearing responsibilities. This has strong implications for philanthopy. We have tended to defer to the male partner as the charitable "decision-maker."

Many organizations don't capitalize on the charitable intents of their female prospects by researching their capabilities and publicizing their gifts to others. According to *Women's Philanthropy*, the newsletter of the National Network on Women as Philanthropists, an investigation conducted by Southwestern University in Georgetown, Texas, revealed that the largest single gift to the university was made by a woman—saving that institution from going under!

Marketing Keys for Reaching Women

■ **Don't treat women like men.**

Men and women don't communicate in the same ways. Their focuses are different.

Content: Men generally talk about money, sports, and business while women generally talk about people, feelings, and relationships.

Style: Men express to fix. Conversation is a competition. Talk to resolve problems. Women, on the other hand, express to understand. Support conversation. They talk to connect with others.

Structure: Men are precise, to the point, without descriptive details. Women tend to be detailed and circuitous.

Building rapport, good listening, and personalization are keys when cultivating and soliciting women donors. Be especially careful not to use peer pressure: While men respond well to the challenge of one-upmanship, it is usually ineffective with women.

■ **Differentiate among women.**

Today's woman doesn't fit into any one grouping. Boomer women differ from their counterparts of 20 years ago. There is more variety among women of similar age groups. Recognize that women are not a homogeneous group. Segment out groupings of particular interest to you. Use demographics of marital history, income, age, and lifestyle. Martha Taylor, founder of the Center for Women and Philanthropy at the University of Wisconsin, proposes the following "unscientific groupings of women":

- Married/Widow—wealthy, older, 75+
- Married/Widow—wealthy, younger, 45+

Gender Differences in Giving

Generally, men give for recognition while women give from the heart.

WOMEN:

- Reasons involving a personal response to need
- Give to specific needs
- Give time and money
- Give because of personal impact
- Personal involvement in organization
- Want to make a difference

MEN:

- Give for recognition
- Giving is reciprocal
- For networking
- Longer tradition of giving money
- Practical, tax-saving reasons
- Business reasons

SOURCE: UCLA study, 1992

- Married/Widow—well to do, never worked at a professional job
- Married/Widow—well to do, works/worked at a professional job
- Single—wealthy, older, 75+
- Single—wealthy, younger, 45+
- Single—well-to-do, never worked at a professional job
- Single—well-to-do, works/worked at a professional job

While Taylor's segmentation is demographically determined, it is logical to assume differing attitudes, values, and lifestyles based on age and history of working/non-working. This can be used to create a "we" feeling.

If you show women in brochures, newsletters, and appeals, know whom you want to attract. The message "I belong" will only work when the role models parallel how a woman feels about herself or wishes to perceive herself as being similar to. If your audience is the mature widow who has inherited money, your photographs must show a background of home and family. Dress is more formal; makeup subdued. If your appeal is aimed at the career woman—self-made, probably younger and possibly never married—your photograph should use an active background of office or a travel setting. Your model's dress should be either a business suit or leisure clothing. You may want to include a cordless phone, VCR, fax, or computer; large numbers of younger, single women have a fascination with gadgets.

More mature women are likely to continue to support charities chosen by spouses or parents. They often are less comfortable "being in charge" than are younger women. Having inherited their wealth, pre-Boomer women may, in fact, welcome your organization's "taking care" of them. Often they are less experienced in finance and, because they trust you, welcome the idea of planned gifts. Successful mature women are good candidates for programs designed to help women succeed in careers and positions of leadership, funding programs for the elderly, and are often in the forefront of environmental movements.

Boomer and Buster women are more likely to be offended by any paternalistic approach. They see themelves as decision-makers, setting a course of action that secures their own future. They are most likely to give locally, where they can see the results of their charity. Baby boom and younger women support social advocacy causes including environmental protection, abortion rights, and arms regulation.

You must constantly reexamine your target group because attitudes, values, and lifestyles are in flux for many women. The late 30s through mid 40s are often a time of reevaluation which can signal changes in priorities. For example, many women in their 40s are beginning to recognize the need for financial planning for retirement and are receptive to looking at planned-giving vehicles.

■ **Recognize that personality—far more so than income, age or marital or career status—determines a woman's financial decisions.** Women who display assertiveness, openness to change, an adventurous spirit and an optimistic outlook are more likely than others to set specific financial goals, save and invest regularly, make retirement planning a priority and educate themselves about money management.

■ **Focus on relationship-building.**

Women tend to volunteer before they give. Acknowledge women's voluntary and in-kind contributions as well as their financial ones.

Women like to collaborate. They enjoy working in groups and view each other as peers. Peer pressure and competition is *not* a female trait.

Women tend to establish connections on an emotional or personal level more quickly than do men. If they don't establish a personal rapport with the solicitor, they won't give.

Women are responsive to nurturing and support. Treated well, they will be eager to tell their network of your fine organization. Their loyalty is uncompromising.

Recognize the need for longer cultivation. Women, in general, take the responsibility of giving money very seriously. They tend to be more conservative in choosing charities. They look for demonstrated fiscal accountability. In making larger gifts, they often favor endowments and/or establishing a charitable foundation.

Be patient. Recognize that many women are more concerned with their ability to replace assets than are men. Making a major gift triggers anxieties.

■ **Recognize women as leaders.**

Show women in your publications. Have photographs of both women and men. Show some women without men. Show women in their late 30s and 40s as well as more mature examples. But don't be offensive. Appealing to women as women, just like targeting specific racial or ethnic groups, must have a logical context and sensitivity.

Be inclusive with your trustees and key committees. Keep abreast of the achievements of entrepreneurial, professional and corporate women in your community. Bring them to the attention of your nominating committee.

Establish a women's advisory council. Role models play a major role in encouraging positive attitudes towards giving. Women will respond—as do men—more positively when solicited by their peers, friends, and colleagues.

■ **Establish your credentials with women.**

According to Shaw and Taylor writing in *Reinventing Fund Raising: Realizing the Potential of Women's Philanthropy:*

> The ability to bring about change and make a difference ranks number one as a motivation for women's giving.

> Women are willing to support new and different causes and prefer to give where their gifts will make a difference. For women, making a difference means making a change rather than preserving the status quo.

An example: Anita Roddick, founder of The Body Shop, an international chain of natural cosmetics stores, has funded projects from Save the Whales to helping the homeless help themselves.

Partner with women's organizations and causes in your community. Identify project areas of particular interest to women. Breast cancer research, the arts and culture, and the environment are among these.

Speak at women's professional groups and write articles for their newsletters.

Visit with women.

- **Be sensitive.**

Make sure you include both the husband and wife in discussions.

Jointly credit all gifts made by couples unless told otherwise. Review your procedures for acknowledgment and gift recording.

Respect salutation and title preferences.

Many women shy away from public recognition. It sets them apart from their community. Respect your prospect's preferences. She may be more willing to provide a gift in tribute or in memory of a loved one rather than directly acknowledging herself.

Within every demographic segmentation—by age, sex, race or ethnic group; by income, education, occupation; using household characteristics, residence, or life stage—women tend to be the target either as direct consumers or as purchasers for others. Check your marketing plan for hidden biases and audit your front line staff for unconscious patronization. No business—whether run by males or females—can afford sexism.

Doris Critz, director of development at Planned Parenthood of New York City, warns that "the changing lifestyles of women, as well as the vanishing myths about what they can and cannot do, demand that we fund raisers change our attitudes and practices. We must give more than lip service to the equal importance and effectiveness of men and women . . . Stereotypes that men and women have about women are breaking down through our society. It's in our best interest to help them disappear. In so doing, we will liberate an important potential for giving and getting."

Do's and Don'ts with Women

Do	Don't
Do address her by name	Don't call her honey, dear, or sweetie
Do treat her with respect	Don't patronize her or talk down to her
Do listen to what she is saying	Don't do all the talking
Do answer *her* if she asks the question	Don't just talk to her husband or male companion
Do project confidence and knowledge	Don't think charm is a substitute for knowledge
Do allow her time to gather information	Don't use high-pressure tactics
Do understand how women network	Don't think of her as a one-time donor
Do realize that women are loyal customers	Don't lose her and her network

SOURCE: *Targeting the New Professional Woman*, Gerry Myers, Probus 1994.

10 Cultural Diversity

Our world is diversifying, racially and ethnically. Cultural diversity is a fact of life in today's—and tomorrow's—society. Diversity can bring innovation, creativity, and better problem solving.

Each geographical area has a different definition of who is the "majority" and who the "minority." This chapter will not attempt to provide demographic and psychographic specifics related to ethnicity or racial background. Rather, it will focus on how we can become inclusive for *all* segments of society.

Your organization needs to begin with an "environmental scan." Working with government census departments, local chambers of commerce, key businesses, and your colleges and universities, develop an accurate picture of your geographic sphere of influence. Then, compare it to the donor makeup of your organization. Do you have representation from the diverse population you serve? Probably not.

Because affluence is found in all segments and sectors of our populations, not-for-profits needs to be as inclusive. **All in-**

dividuals need to feel their participation is genuinely welcome and valued. Your organization may not be perceived by the ethnic communities as welcoming.

Appreciating Diversity

If we could, at this very moment, shrink the earth's population to a village of precisely 100—but maintain the existing human ratios—it would look like this:

57	Asians
21	Europeans
14	Western Hemispheric People (North and South Americans)
8	Africans
70	Non-white
30	White
70	Unable to read
50	Malnourished
80	Living in substandard housing
1	University graduate

50% of the entire world's wealth would be in the hands of 6 people—all citizens of the United States.

SOURCE: International Fund Raising Workshop, 1994.

Do the staff, trustees, and key volunteer committees reflect the diversity of the populations you serve and wish to attract as donors? For many charities, the honest answer is "no."

There are four key areas that not-for-profits need to examine:

l. Formal qualifications for participation: They may be exclusive or have financial/occupational restrictions. Few minorities are persons of wealth. They may not be able to make the largest gifts on your board. But, if they can't bring "wealth," they can bring "wisdom and work."

Prospective staff may not have the formal educational credentials you seek. Or they may have attended schools you've never heard of. Be flexible.

2. An organizational inability to assess the "talent pool" of minorities: Traditionally, we've looked for leadership in the corporate sector. Many minorities are not making it in corporate life. The problem is not simply one of racism. There are few role models, few means by which even ambitious people of color can rise. They often choose to run their own businesses because they are intimidated by lack of access to the corporate "club."

3. A refusal to recruit aggressively: The majority of not-for-profit organizations have not been proactive. To involve minorities, you must make an explicit commitment to increase minority participation and make special efforts to recruit minorities. To find persons of color possessing the qualifications you desire in a trustee, you must seek out networking opportunities at professional meetings, social and church events.

- Make direct contact with minority communities. Demonstrate your respect for the diversity within your local ethnic communities by participating in or co-sponsoring festivals and celebrations. Festivals, fairs, and other community events draw large crowds and provide an ideal opportunity to build awareness for your organization.
- Recruit one-on-one. Regularly make use of alternative media and community-based organizations for identification of up-and-coming minorities. Ethnically targeted magazines regularly run articles with biographical information on upwardly-mobile men and women in a variety of communities. Several publications run yearly lists of individuals who are doing well in a variety of occupations. Most publications have regular features, such as a newsmaker's column, which list accomplishments and promotions.

Once you've found an individual who interests your organization, write or telephone. Refer to the article or listing that caught your attention so your potential candidate knows that you proactively reach into his or her community. But don't insult the individual by making race or ethnic background the sole criteria for your interest in him or her: explain what qualities you think he or she will contribute to the charity as a successful businessperson or community leader. *While contributing to the diversity of viewpoints is also valid, it should never be the only reason.*

4. Avoid cultural insensitivity. Cultural differences make recruitment of minorities difficult for non-minority management. Often organizations fail to recognize:

- stereotypes and their associated assumptions
- actual cultural differences
- exclusivity of the "white male club" and its associated access to important information and relationships
- unwritten rules and double standards for success which are often unknown to women and minorities
- lack of communication about differences

Affluence is found in all segments and sectors. However, cultures differ. You must market according to the specifics of the culture of the individual you wish to cultivate.

To design a successful fund-raising program for ethnic and minority markets, you must take cultural differences into consideration. Marlene Rossman, writing in *Multicultural Marketing*, enumerates these keys to consider:

■ **High- and Low-Context Cultures:** Communication in a high-context culture depends heavily on the context, or nonverbal aspects of communication; low-context cultures depend more on explicit, verbally expressed communcation. Much of Europe, North America, and Australia are low-context cultures, relying heavily on information communicated explicitly by words. Asian, South American, Middle Eastern, and African cultures, by contrast, are high-context.

■ **Nonverbal Communication:** Different cultures interpret gestures, facial expressions, eye contact, body language, and silence in different ways. These can be easily misinterpreted by outsiders. For example, most children in the United Kingdom are taught to look at the teacher or parent when they are being scolded. In many Asian, Latin Amcrican, Caribbean, and other cultures, in contrast, children are often expected to look down or away as a sign of respect for the person who is chas tising them. As adults, the British think someone who doesn't look them in the eye is shifty or untrustworthy; most Asians, however, think that looking someone in the eye is rude or confrontational.

Body space is another area of difference. People who live in high-contact cultures, including Mediterranean, Latin American, and Middle Eastern countries, typically stand about a foot apart when they interact, face each other directly, and engage in lots of eye contact and touching. At the other end of the continuum are Northern European cultures where people stand farther apart and try to avoid accidental touching in social and business settings.

■ **Communicating in a foreign language:** This is one of the most basic considerations. If you decide to translate your appeals, brochures, newsletters, and program materials into another language make sure the translation is correct for the subsection you want to reach. And, be careful: "common" words can take on a meaning very different from what you mean. The Chevy Nova literally translated as "no go" in Spanish, heavily impacting on that car's sales!

■ **Individualism:** Some cultures emphasize the "I" consciousness, in which identity is rooted mostly in the self, compared to the "we" consciousness, in which a person's identity is rooted in groups. Latin American cultures and, to varying degrees, Asian cultures focus more on the group than the individual.

Also keep in mind:

■ **Formality:** Do not use a person's first name until and unless a relationship has been established.

■ **Rank, Hierarchy, and Tradition:** In many cultures, older is better. And preserving dignity and saving face are extremely important.

■ **Colors, Numbers, and Symbols:** Some are considered lucky and others unlucky. While Americans consider the number 13 unlucky, it is the number 4 that Asians consider cursed.

If we truly understand the changing face of our world, then we must demonstrate that we value diversity. Organizations must show by our actions that we applaud and appreciate that individuals are different and that these differences are not to be simply tolerated but must be encouraged, supported, and nurtured.

In the United States, the Hispanic, black and Asian populations present special opportunities and challenges. U.S. fund raisers interested in these audiences will find relevant material in my books *Changing Demographics* and *Pinpointing Affluence*.

Part III

Changing Development Strategies

Not-for-profits and charities have lagged far behind businesses in understanding how the changes in our population and technology lead our donors and prospects to expect different marketing methodologies. In the next chapters, we'll explore how to place the demographic and psychographic information of parts one and two in a strategic framework.

11 Changing Fund-Raising Strategies

When the Paradigm Shifts, Everyone Goes Back to Zero

Because the *who* has changed, the *how* must change as well.

The increasing longevity and diversity of our populations change people's response to technology and, in turn, will change the way we do fund raising in fundamental ways. Different life experiences mean that our donors and prospects will lack common life "triggers." Their philanthropic personalities and attitudes toward money will not be the same. The differences mean we will need to do more "intergenerational" marketing.

Too many of us still work under the old paradigms: assuming we can access an unlimited pool of donors, treating all donors and prospects as if they share common "generational anchors," and ignoring changing—often preferred—methodologies and technologies for both marketing and fulfillment.

At the beginning of this book, I listed the changing fund-raising paradigms.

Because your donors and prospects are living longer:

- Concentrate on renewal and upgrading donors rather than on the acquisition of new prospects
- Prepare to receive major gift income through planned gifts and legacies rather than through current giving

Because the majority of today's adults were born after World War II, not before:

- Don't expect automatic donor loyalty
- Suggest meaningful levels of giving: US $100 or UK £75 as opposed to US $25 or UK £10 to "make a difference"

Let's look at each changing paradigm in turn:

Because your donors and prospects are living longer:

■ Concentrate on renewal and upgrading donors rather than on the acquisition of new prospects

In the 1970s and 1980s there were always more and more new prospects. This was because, during those years, wave after wave of Baby Boomers reached adulthood. When the baby boom ended, so did the ever increasing pool of new prospects. From the mid-1990s and beyond, we're dealing with a much smaller group of new adults for acquisition. And we get to deal with the same prospects, over and over again. Length of life is increasing dramatically even as numbers of "new" adults are decreasing.

The median age of our population is moving past 40. In 1980, the first of the Baby Boomers turned 40. As the massive Boomer cohort moved from young adulthood to middle age, the traditional population pyramid bulged in the middle.

- During the 1950s - 1970s, we had a large number of children and teenagers, a middling number of young through 40s adults, and a very small grouping of mature adults and the elderly, forming the traditional population pyramid.

- In the 1980s through 2000, the pyramid's base of Boomers are moving into their adult years and, as a result, the population pyramid "bulged" in the middle and became a rectangle.
- And, because people can only get older, as we move into the 21st century, our rectangle becomes top-heavy with older individuals. The population pyramid inverts.

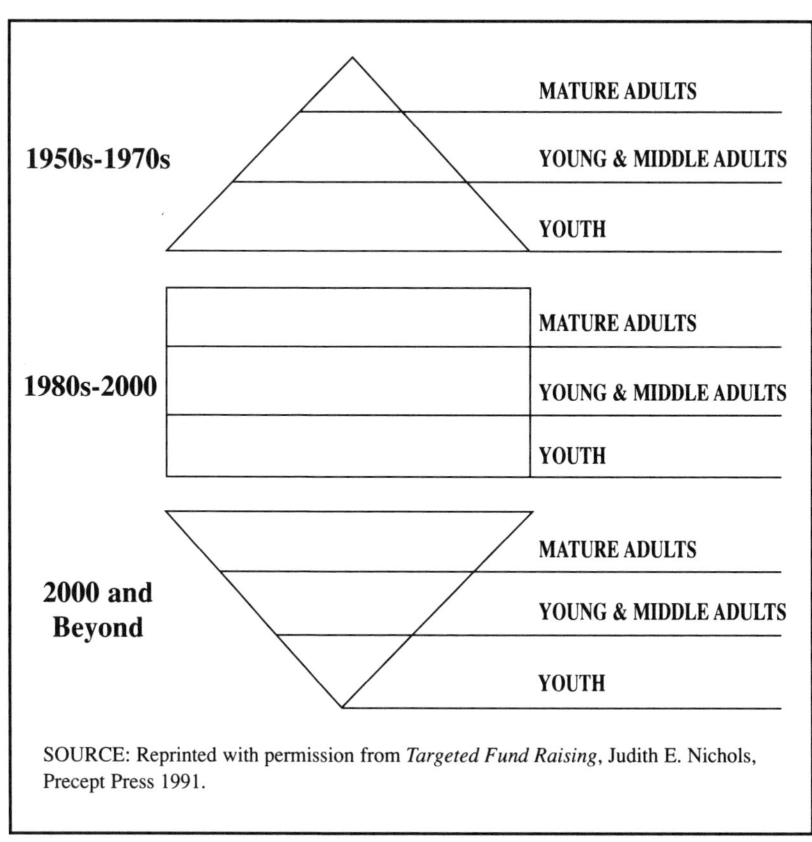

SOURCE: Reprinted with permission from *Targeted Fund Raising*, Judith E. Nichols, Precept Press 1991.

***Fifty years from now, when middle-aging Baby Boomers join the ranks of the elderly, the old may outnumber the young.* If you don't work hard now to retain your best donors, you won't be able to replace them with new ones.**

As more and more people live longer and longer, their lifelong value to your organization grows as well. Because of their increasing longevity, the donor you attract at age 40 will—with proper cultivation and donor relationship-building activities—continue to give, year after year at upgraded levels, for 30, 40, 50 or more years. Hopefully, your organization will receive the ultimate gift as well: a bequest.

Creating this life-long "bonding" requires that we thoroughly rethink the way we do business. For most not-for-profits the focus has been on acquisition of donors, not renewal. Flipping our philosophy to an aftermarketing focus requires a restructuring of resources, time, and values.*

■ Prepare to receive major gift income through planned gifts and legacies rather than through current giving

The fastest growing age groups are the oldest ones. Of all the people who have lived to age 65 in the history of the world, more than half are alive today. Fifty years from now, when middle-aging Baby Boomers join the ranks of the elderly, the old may outnumber the young.

- Our elderly populations are growing twice or more as fast as total populations.
- Women outlive men by an average of seven years, making our older populations increasingly female.
- The elderly tend to live alone.

It takes about 15 years for our perceptions to catch up with reality. Most of us are just beginning to understand the implications of our increasing longevity. But, increasingly, we do. With that acceptance will come an understandable reluctance to part with assets that might be needed to sustain lifestyles and handle the threat of end-of-life medical needs. The capital campaign of today will give way to the endowment campaign of tomorrow.

Fund raisers need to begin preparing for tomorrow's logical resistance to current, sacrifical giving today. Because it typically

---

* The need to do a better job of renewal and upgrading is addressed in depth in my book *Growing from Good to Great* (Bonus Books 1995) which focuses on aftermarketing strategies for fund raisers.

What Are Your Donors Expecting from Their Gifts?

While the heart prompts the mind to give, your not-for-profit must clearly articulate to potential contributors the benefits it provides in three key areas:

- Addressing core needs: Each donor has an agenda he or she wants addressed. There are five leading niches (the home, education, health and fitness, leisure time, and finances).

  Example: a desire to combat aging

- Packaging: Once the core need is identified, the individual evaluates how well various options might meet that need. This can be accomplished through a purchase or donation.

  Example: Buy cosmetics (short-term purchase solution), have plastic surgery (long-term purchase solution), join a gym, health club or YMCA (active solution), fund medical research (societal solution), or keep busy through volunteerism (mind-over-body solution).

- Warranties and guarantees: Which path works best? The individual evaluates each package for credibility. Your organization's years of experience, testimonials from both recipients and donors, and recognition by the community and media all provide the necessary reassurances that attest to your organizational worth and create donor loyalty.

takes three to five years for a legacy and planned giving program to begin producing, it's especially important to put a strong program in place now.

Another thought: By creating a steady stream of legacies and planned gifts your organization will actually have a more stable base of support in the future.

Because the majority of adults were born after World War II, not before:

- Don't expect automatic donor loyalty.

While the majority of individuals give to charity every year, few have a single priority. The typical individual donates to 11 to 14 charities each year and often cannot differentiate between one good organization in the field and another. In addition, increasingly, options exist for meeting the donor's needs, goals, and objectives in the world of business: Never before have our constituents faced so many choices.

Notes Jenny Thompson of Craver, Mathews, Smith: ". . . Corporations—painfully and expensively—have finally come to understand that the old concepts of 'mass marketing,' 'customer loyalty,' and 'brand loyalty' have gone the way of Pan American airlines, Macy's Department Store, Sears and even venerable IBM. Consumers are now better informed . . . have access to far more information . . . are de-

Behind Boomers' Growing Dissatisfaction

Much of the Boomers' skepticism and lack of loyalty has been developed or reinforced by their workplace experience. Among these:

- Move away from major companies with their stability and toward smaller, less "secure" employment.
- The social contract between employer and employee has been broken, resulting in the death of lifetime employment.
- The need to survive has overtaken the desire to provide safe harbor, unless corporations can be persuaded that such loyalty to employees results in bottom-line results, long and short term.

SOURCE: *Future Tense: The Business Realities of the Next Ten Years*, Ian Morrison and Greg Schmid, William Morrow & Co. 1994.

manding more information . . . and show their loyalty only to those who provide good information and high-quality service."

A key characteristic of Baby Boomers—the largest of our adult population groupings—is a growing alienation from and falling confidence in leadership. All their lives, Boomers have had to compete for resources and recognition. As a result, they have grown up distrustful of institutions and unwilling to be taken for granted. Boomers and younger adults tend to be less forgiving of poor service and more unwilling to be taken for granted; less tolerant of mistakes and mismanagement by and within our organizations; and more impatient to have their concerns addressed promptly and properly.

With today's middle-aging and younger adults *there is no second chance*. You must deliver every time and constantly recultivate. You need to find ways to integrate the donor into your organization, to create and sustain a relationship that "bonds" customer to not-for-profit.

- Suggest meaningful levels of giving: US $100 or UK £75 as opposed to US $25 and UK £10 to "make a difference."

When it comes to making discretionary purchases, we all go back to our childhood memories of what money was worth. Charitable gifts—like leisure activities and the small luxuries of life (a splurge on chocolate or the purchase of the latest novel)—are often decided impulsively. Because they are not "must do" purchases (such as food, clothing, and shelter), the purchaser must feel good about the expenditure.

The majority of our adult population grew up in inflationary times. While Pre- and World War II audiences tend to continue to believe that US $25 or UK £10 is a meaningful level of giving, those born from 1946 on see US $100 or UK £75 as having the same buying power. *Don't ask for too little.*

The paradigms are changing and we must change with them. As we move ahead into the new century you will need to segment not only your prospect audiences, but also your fund-raising methodologies and your fulfillment options.

The marketing matrix for methodologies and fulfillment will look somewhat like this:

AUDIENCE	FUND-RAISING METHODOLOGY	FULFILLMENT OPTION
Mature Donors (50 years and older)	Face to face, Direct mail	Checks or one-time gifts of assets made during life via planned giving as well as bequests
Middle-Aged Donors (30 to 50 years)	Face to face, Telephone, Video	Pledges over time and one-time gifts via credit cards; Major gifts via bequest only
Younger Donors (18 to 30 years)	Internet	Continuous gifts via electronic fund transfer and bank draft; use of debit cards rather than credit cards, little hope of major gifts

Once you understand the broad strategic implications of changing demographics and technologies, your organization must adopt specific developmental plans that address the issues, concerns, and opportunities the new paradigms raise.

According to Ken Burnett, the author of *Relationship Fundraising*, you will need to focus on:

- Establishing comprehensive, usable donor histories
- Forming lasting relationships with donors
- Evaluating donors objectively
- Acquiring new donors at acceptable cost levels

- Developing an integrated approach to donor communication
- Segmenting our donor files
- Giving our donors choices
- Encouraging donors to give more, more regularly
- Making giving by bequest irresistible
- Adapting to new government requirements

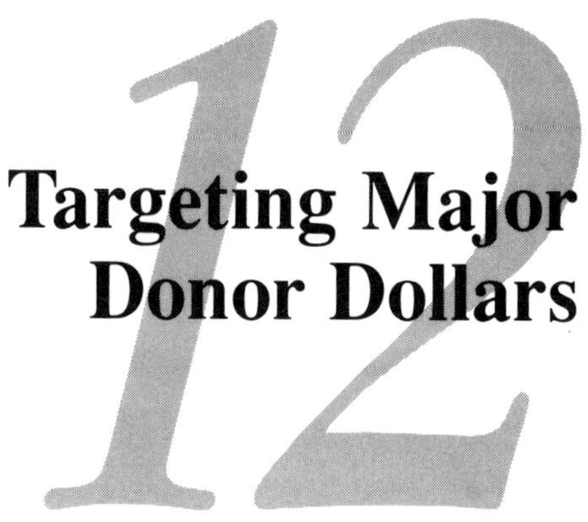

12 Targeting Major Donor Dollars

It would be wonderful if everyone you identified as a prospect for fund raising could be cultivated and solicited face-to-face. That's the most effective form of fund raising.

But for most organizations, that's simply not realistic. Given a wealth (no pun intended) of current donors and logical prospects, we need to make hard choices about who is a priority and who is not. That determines who will be handled more personally and who receives only direct mail.

By working from the "center out"
and from the "top down"
you can easily identify the prospects
who should be your organization's priority.

Working from the "Center Out"

Consciously start your major gift fund raising with those closest to your organization, committing the greatest share of your time, energy and resources to those who are most likely to understand and support your cause. Initially, concentrate your visits on:

- Trustees and fund-raising development committee members
- Members of the staff
- Current donors
- Current volunteers
- Current members
- Retired trustees
- Retired staff
- Past donors (especially LYBUTS—last year but not this year and SYBUTS—some year but not this year)
- Past volunteers
- Alumni and past members

When you've gone through those lists—using the input of your fund-raising committee, trustees and staff as well as public databases and your local media—you may not need, initially, to go any further to identify your first top 25. But, if you do, choose additional prospects from:

- Those who attend your programs or special events
- Those who buy products or services affiliated with your organization
- Those who are "related" (parents, grandparents, other family members or close friends) to your closest supporters

Working from the "Top Down"

A "quick and dirty" way of determining who belongs at the top of your list for cultivation and solicitation is to run two lists of your organization's supporters. The first list identifies all donors for the last complete fiscal year (and/or current year if you are far enough along to use this year as the benchmark) in descending order—largest single gift-giver first, proceeding down to the smallest gift-giver last. The second list uses the same format but gives the cumulative giving histories of current and past donors, going back as far as you believe useful and/or accurate.

A more sophisticated method, suggested by Ken Burnett, would be to assign points for recency, frequency, and monetary value of gifts. You can vary the points and values to suit your organization so long as they remain consistent for all donors.

Recency

- Award eight points to a donor who donated within the last six months
- Award four points to a donor who donated six to 12 months ago
- Award two points to a donor who donated 12–24 months ago
- Award one point to a donor who last donated more than two years ago

Frequency

- Take the number of donations and multiply by four points

Value

- Award one point for every US $50 (UK £25) to a maximum of 40 points

SOURCE: *Relationship Fundraising*, Ken Burnett, White Lion Press 1992.

Use Psychographics for Major Donor Cultivation

Once you've put together a list of individuals capable of making larger gifts, you need to understand the "triggers" that can move prospects along. The relationship between the fund raiser and the major gifts prospect cannot be adversarial. In seeking to match up a potential donor with a project or program that addresses his or her area of concern, we look for "win-win" situations. In a sense, once the prospect expresses interest, the development officer must sit on the "same side of the table," working as much for the prospect as for the organization the fund raiser represents.

This "voluntary exchange of benefits," cited by Philip Kotler in *Marketing for Nonprofit Organizations*, is marketing. No matter how worthy, your organization's needs and goals will not call forth support from the private sector unless the needs and goals of the potential donor are equally met.

Not-for-profits have become increasingly sophisticated at articulating missions, goals, and objectives in ways that facilitate this exchange. Using psychographics, the fund raiser can pinpoint the values, attitudes, and lifestyle particulars that will determine the general type of program/project the potential donor is likely to find of interest and the best time in the lifecycle of a program/project to involve him or her. This can be the key to quicker decision-making on the part of the major gift prospect.

While there are numerous formal psychographic assessments you can use to match donor and project, most charities do not have either the financial resources to pay for the most sophisticated screening packages. While you can do this yourself utilizing surveys, many not-for-profits are reluctant to press prospects and donors to actively cooperate. Is it realistic to go to "Mr. Jones" and ask: "Please check off your likes and dislikes on this survey so I can do a better job of soliciting you?" Instead, consider using my "quick and dirty" personality assessment theory described below.

Nichols' Personality Theory

Looking for more significant gifts and a quicker close? You can use the visible "clues" that donors and prospects provide to predict contributors' and prospective donors' most likely areas of funding interest and willingness to take risks.

Start by visualizing a bell-shaped curve. The majority of your prospects will fall within the center of the curve. Let's call these individuals "members of the herd." Those we can place to the extreme left, we'll call "innovators." Those to the extreme right, let's call "laggards." (While I developed this theory initially for use with individuals, it is equally valid for trusts and businesses.)

Clues to a prospect's personality will be found by examining her or his:

- History of contributions to your organization and other charities (What type of project? What stage of the project?)
- Lifestyle choices (Type of car? Travel destinations? Style of dressing? Preferred entertainment?)
- Choice of profession
- Residence type and location
- Stage of life (children at home, mid-life childless, retiree)

Let's look at the three kinds of personalities:

■ **Innovators** look to be in the forefront. They want the opportunity to set new directions, to encourage others, to play a leadership role. They are often idealistic and impulsive. Innovators expect to be approached by representatives of stature. They are good prospects for the untried: they like experimental and pilot programs and are willing to fund riskier projects.

Innovators have high opinions of themselves. It often takes a highly-placed, well-regarded peer to provide an introduction. However, once the contact has been made, innovators are willing to work with staff—as long as the development officer clearly has decision-making authority.

Innovators need to be involved in the planning process and often enjoy playing an active role with the organizations they support. Never approach innovators with a formalized document. They like feeling that they are getting a "first look" and that there is room for their input. Draft documents and photocopied memos, sketches rather than formal graphics, unmounted photos rather than a glossy brochure—this is what innovators look for.

An articulate spokesperson can quickly ignite innovators' enthusiasm but, often, they have short attention spans. They show little loyalty and will move on to other organizations if a new project or program catches their attention. While you may find the initial meeting to be very encouraging, beware! The relationship with an innovator can deteriorate rapidly if he or she doesn't feel you take him or her seriously. Innovators expect you to anticipate requests, provide immediate follow-up and extraordinary service.

Innovators go on instinct. They "like" a project or they don't. Because they view themselves as the busiest of individuals, don't waste their time. Push for quick decision-making on their part.

Because innovators see themselves as unique, traditional donor recognition does not appeal to them. They want to be acknowledged, but the vehicle must be as bold as themselves. Visibility and publicity are usually very important to innovators. They aren't shy about suggesting what they would like. Many innovators keep scrapbooks; they may laminate their press clippings and display them proudly.

Tax benefits matter to the innovator, more as a demonstration of how to "work the system" to one's best advantage rather than as a need. Often, an innovator will explore more complicated vehicles for gift-giving just because the mechanics appeal to her or him!

■ **Members of the herd,** unlike the bold innovator, need to be reassured that—while their support will make a significant difference to your charity—their contributions are being used for more conventional programs and projects. Members of the herd are often willing to furnish the gifts that enlarge an existing program or provide for a more advanced stage of a successful project. They don't want to be approached before the plan has been thought through and approved by the board and the community.

Formal documents are important to members of the herd, demonstrating organizational commitment and endorsement. The glossy brochure is reassuring to them.

Herd members look for peer approval. They want to be part of the "in" crowd. If a respected individual makes a significant gift, members of the herd will quickly follow. A challenge campaign will interest them.

Herd prospects respond best when appeals are made by a higher-placed friend or business colleague. The fund raiser must take a back seat in the cultivation and solicitation process, serving as a facilitator to the volunteer or organization's CEO.

While innovators tend to laugh at traditional recognition vehicles, members of the herd take visible signs of their contributions very seriously. Donor club membership cards, attractive plaques, and naming walls on buildings are expected by herd members. Such interests provide a visual clue to their personality: If you are visiting the home or office of a prospect and find the walls covered with citations and plaques, you are definitely visiting a member of the herd!

■ **Laggards** take their time deciding whether or not to support your organization. They are cautious, looking for visible signs of success (positive articles in the press, letters of endorsement) before making the commitment.

Laggards like to invest in tangibles: equipment, bricks and mortar. Endowments appeal to them. They want to know your organization has already made a significant commitment itself for part of the program or project's funding from its operating budget. Laggards are good candidates for bequests and other planned gifts.

Usually, laggards are not concerned about recognition. In fact, they are often offended by the perceived cost of tangible gifts and givebacks. Laggards don't seek publicity and often prefer to make their gifts anonymously. They are sincerely surprised that your organization wants to honor them for doing what is their duty.

Laggards see themselves as simple folks. They do not expect to have lunch with the organization's CEO; they prefer to deal with the fund raiser. They hesitate to be "trouble."

Fund raisers often find laggards frustrating because these individuals seem to take forever to make up their minds to support your organization. But, once a laggard decides to include you, he or she is the most loyal and generous of donors. Laggards often progress from the modest "test" gift to larger annual contributions and legacies.

Recognizing Organizational Personalities

Like your prospects, your organization has a personality type. And, while your agency's or institution's leadership may assume that the mission statement has neatly pegged your not-for-profit as "innovative," a careful look at your programs and projects—those you are currently offering, those you have dropped for lack of interest or funding, those you are targeting for the future—may provide a startling insight as to the personality clues you are actually providing to potential funders.

It is not uncommon to find that a charity with a very bold, idealistic mission statement actually takes a conservative approach to saving the world.

Conversely, many times the not-for-profit with a cautiously expressed case statement takes on the riskier programs. Often an internal analysis by staff and board is needed to resolve the conflicts between rhetoric and reality. Bringing volunteers, trustees, and staff (program, administrative and fund raising) into the process can lead to everyone having a firmer understanding of your agency's interpretation of its mission.

Seek a "Personality Match" between Donor and Organization

Making the most effective use of Nichols' Personality Theory requires that the fund raiser recognize the psychographics of both the organization and the donor.

> **You should seek a match between prospect and proposal, reflecting a commonality of attitude based on whether both sides are stressing innovation or security.**

A secondary consideration is the timing of the appeal: At what stage of a project's development (initial, ongoing, maturity) will there be greatest interest on the part of a particular donor? At what stage of development does the organization need funds most urgently?

Various scenarios will suggest themselves:

- That you have a strong match betwen prospects and proposals and can go ahead with confidence.
- That your prospects fall clearly toward one end of the spectrum and your proposals are clustered at the other end, suggesting you will need to identify either new prospects or proposals.
- That the general clustering for both prospects and proposals is close, but you need to do some "massaging" to help prospects see the match.

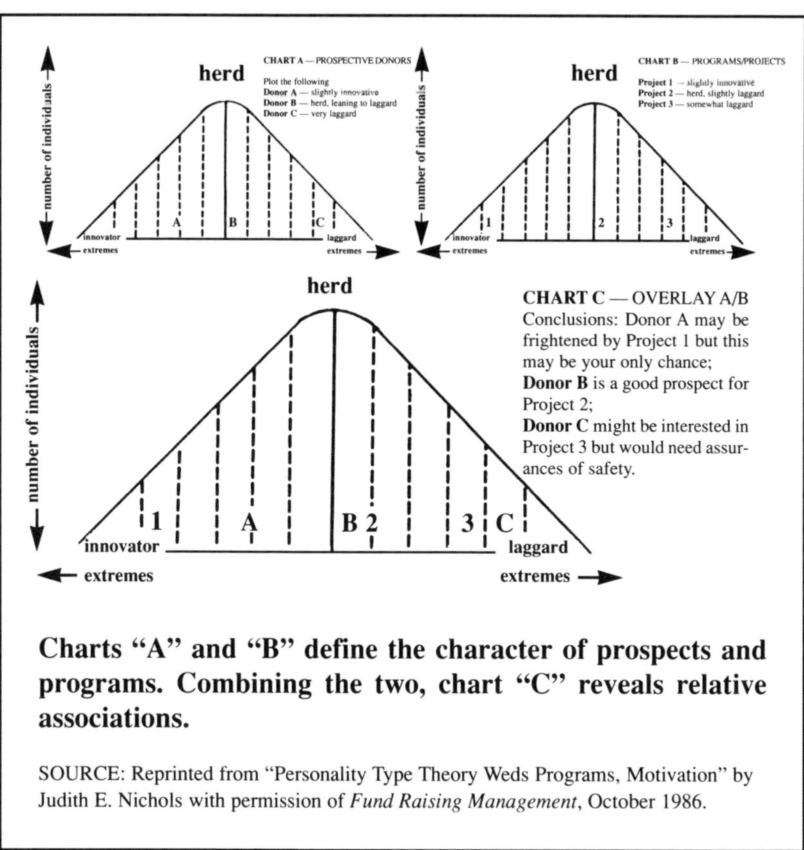

Charts "A" and "B" define the character of prospects and programs. Combining the two, chart "C" reveals relative associations.

SOURCE: Reprinted from "Personality Type Theory Weds Programs, Motivation" by Judith E. Nichols with permission of *Fund Raising Management*, October 1986.

Laying one bell-shaped graph over the other, as in the illustration above, allows you to see which prospects and proposals match most closely.

Using the Personality Theory for Fund Raising

By taking the time to analyze the compatibility of prospects and proposals, the fund raiser shows a sincere interest in the personality of the prospect.

I always tell prospects that the initial meeting is to "get acquainted." I explain our organization's concern about linking interests and needs so we can forge the strongest of relationships. I stress that such a linkage must provide satisfaction to both sides, and I invite the prospect to help me on her or his behalf by letting me know if my analysis of her or his personality type is accurate.

I invite prospects to help me by indicating how they view themselves in terms of innovation and timing. Prospects respond well to this approach, often enlarging upon my initial analysis or correcting my perceptions.

If I have been correct in my initial assumptions I can introduce a specific program or project. If not, I can involve the prospect actively in identifying two or three possibilities for consideration. I make an appointment to return with full information in either case. *We work as partners rather than as adversaries.*

A Case Example

"Bob Smith" was a trustee at a major university. Each year, he made a $1,000 gift for scholarships—promptly but without ever increasing the amount. Yet, I knew he was extremely wealthy and, in his own words, would "one day endow a scholarship fund"—the traditional laggard gift.

I arranged to visit with Bob, hoping to find some clues to his personality type. His office was simply decorated—no plaques, traditional furniture; his style of dress was equally understated.

Immediately, Bob expressed concern for taking up my time and presented me with his annual gift of $1,000. I thanked him, then said: "Bob, we appreciate your support, but I'm concerned. I don't see either joy or satisfaction in your making this gift."

He was startled. I explained that our university felt it was important that both donor and institution benefit from the charitable transaction and that part of my job—why I had asked to visit with him today—was to make sure that the contributor felt good about making the gift. I added, candidly, that this was just good business; we wanted a long-term relationship that would grow.

I invited Bob to talk about himself. What had given him a good feeling lately? He didn't hesitate, telling me about having arranged temporary work for two men from a local shelter. He had taken an active role in making the arrangements and felt good about changing, even slightly, the direction of their lives.

Our conversation revealed that Bob Smith was innovative in scope but a laggard in timing! We addressed both by offering him the chance to challenge a group of younger persons by guaranteeing them scholarships if they made it through secondary school.

13

Segmenting Donors for the Annual Gift

While fund raisers delight in trading stories about the "once-in-a-lifetime" major gifts they have secured, most will acknowledge that consistent, modest annual gifts assure the health of their organizations—providing the current unrestricted income so necessary for essential day-to-day operations as well as paving the way for major and planned giving.

Don't assume that donor loyalty is the norm:

Many organizations make an erroneous assumption that donor loyalty is standard. Once the prospect makes a gift, the charity relaxes—believing it has aquired an annual donor. The major societal shifts make such an assumption dangerous.

■ **Baby Boomers are the least "brand loyal" of our population cohorts.** This stems from their life-long competition for resources and recognition. Having been told since childhood they were special yet having faced the realities of overcrowding in every aspect of their personal and professional lives, Boomers tend to seek out reassurances that you see them as special. They expect you to treat them as unique even when their level of involvement with your charity is modest! Boomers expect organizations seeking their patronage to cultivate them extensively.

■ **Similar tales of "lack of loyalty" are found in other audience segments as well.** The changing role of today's woman—from homemaker to partner or provider of the family's income—has contributed to a swing in the charities they support. Traditionally, women tended to see their wealth as a trust and continued the charitable directions of their husbands and/or fathers. No more! As women earn their own incomes, they are choosing charities that more closely meet their interests.

Mature individuals, once the bastion of loyalty, are also less stable. While the oldest of our populations tend to honor their philanthropic commitments, death is thinning their ranks. And many older persons question whether they can afford to be generous. With the fastest-growing segments of our populations being those over age 85, many fear outliving their assets. As a result they may pull back from current charitable giving.

Not-for-profits and charities have lagged far behind businesses in understanding how the changes in our population and the changes in technology have lead our donors and prospects to expect different methodologies.

Today, you can have your own version of virtually any product. Our overeager embracing of direct response vehicles may, in fact, have contributed to a backlash of resistance among today's more sophisticated prospects. Our donors are not fooled by the marvels of computerization into believing "this message is just for you."

Information technology hardly changed at all until radio and television came along. Over the next 20 years, many experts believe that the information technology may change more than it has over the last 200 years:

- Everyone wants to know more about everything.
- Increased pace causes need for more information, faster.

Don Peppers and Martha Rogers, writing in *The One to One Future: Building Relationships One Customer at a Time*, caution that "The old paradigm, a system of mass production, mass media, and mass marketing, is being replaced by a totally new paradigm, a one-to-one economic system." Economies of scale will never again be as important as they are today.

John Gorman, senior vice president of Epsilon, agrees that the increasingly affordable economics of communication and technology are driving this technological shift:

- less direct mail because of its high cost
- increasing flexibility of the printed medium
- availability of interactive media

Mal Warwick, writing in *Technology and the Future of Fundraising*, predicts that "the business of direct mail fund raising is changing in genuinely fundamental ways under the onslaught of new technologies—inter-networking, "multimedia," wireless communications, etc. Our appeals will need to be individualized, multi-sensory, information-rich, immediate, interactive, and communal."

Your Message is Competing with Information Overload:

The majority of homes have cable TV, with an average of 51 channels per home

There are over 2,400 consumer magazine titles

Increasingly, homes have a personal computer

Over 70% of individuals have shopped by phone or mail

Time Magazine now produces over 100 versions each week

There are over 20 different interactive systems in various stages of testing

SOURCE: *Beyond 2000: The Future of Direct Marketing*, Jerry I. Reitman, NTC Business Books 1994.

■ **The new commandment of Information-Age Marketing:** "Tell, tell, tell, before you start to sell, sell, sell." Baby Boomers have been called "information junkies." They want specific information on the issues that interest them. However, they are too sophisticated to respond to intense, emotional appeals.

Low-key "telling" is going to increasingly replace high-pressure "selling" as the most effective way to get through to jaded consumers as we move further along in the shift from mass marketing to individualized marketing.

There is a major paradigm shift around financial technology:

Mid-life individuals and younger adults are letting go of checks and cash. More and more of us use cards and computers to pay bills, including gifts to charity. This is good news for not-for-profits: it is looking at the checkbook balance that keeps gift amounts low! Few of us are comfortable writing a single large check for charity. Not because we don't care, but rather because we think we can't afford the gesture.

Both Depression and World War II Babies tend to be cash payers, distrusting new technologies. These are the generations that still tuck emergency cash into wallets and handbags. Many prefer a "hands on" arrangement with bill paying and are uncomfortable using ATMs and other "modern" technologies. They are most likely to choose one-time check writing. Major gift giving to them means selling or giving away an asset: solid, real gifts.

Depression and World War II Babies tend to listen to society's recommendations and like to support traditional, well-established charities. Your mature donors will continue to prefer traditional methods of fund raising and fulfillment. Those over-50 are the most literate individuals and actually enjoy receiving well-done direct mail.

Boomers and younger persons grew up in a different world. They tend to prefer the "cashless society," using credit cards, standing orders, and electronic transfers. Our younger donors are the heaviest users of debit cards: nearly one-quarter (24%) of people age 18-23 have debit cards, as do 22% of those age 35-54; only 12% of age 55 or older respondents have them, according to a Gallup survey.

As they accept that their lifespan is likely to take them well into their 90s, few will make major gifts from assets. Major gift giving will take place by bequest instead. To pay for gifts: time payments—just like they pay for everything else—is the preferred methodology. Their gift fulfillment needs to be structured to allow for a constant stream of extremely modest gift amounts.

To make your annual campaign work, personalize the vehicle to the audience. Here are three approaches to consider:

Upgrade Direct Response Mail (Mature Donors)

Older individuals are the most direct mail responsive of our audiences. They have faith in our institutions and often see direct mail as "an invitation to adventure." How do you differentiate your message from the clutter in the mailbox?

The San Diego Zoo in California decided that "cheap is out," and uses expensive mailings which cost between $3.50 and $4 per piece to move first-time members to higher donor tiers. According to Epsilon, the consulting company which formulated the San Diego Zoo's approach, "packages like these mailed to the right audiences are very cost-effective for a wide variety of groups. Epsilon has guided the zoo's direct mail campaign for more than 15 years.

Members receive mail from the zoo at least 16 times a year. Not all pieces are solicitations. *ZOONOOZ*, a monthly, four-color magazine with in-depth reports on the facility's residents, and *Zoo Log*, a quarterly newsletter detailing activities and special events, reinforce the partnership between members and the zoo. Similarly, a "membership appreciation brochure"—with coupons for free rides on the aerial tram and complimentary admission to the children's zoo—tell supporters they count.

The renewal notices and the publications encourage people to become involved in the zoo's mission, ensuring the survival of some of the world's rarest animals.

The zoo sponsors several higher-level membership clubs with distinctive logos and identifications. These clubs stress exclusivity: members receive R.S.V.P. invitations to renew or join a higher-level club, and they receive "privileges" instead of "benefits." Mailings are oriented more toward a feeling of partnership with zoo staff members and less toward free passes and parking and various types of discounts. Club members get "insider" information, certificates of appreciation, and identification pins in the mail.

In addition to its regular membership and club appeals, the zoo does holiday and special-gift appeals. Each reinforces the "we" feeling. The thick holiday package, mailed in October, encourages members to purchase first-level memberships for friends and family. Attractive cards, announcing the gift, are enclosed. The special-gift appeals help the zoo's fund-raising staff identify contributors at the top of the donating ladder: those who can be targeted for legacy gifts.

The key to the success of the San Diego Zoo's direct mail is the organization's willingness to create a feeling of partnership.

Telecommunications Appeals (Mid-life Donors)

Today's mid-life individual (the Baby Boom generation born between 1946 and 1964) has a different informational profile. Raised in the era of television, he or she is impatient with slower methods of receiving information and suspicious of direct mail as well. Videos (still rarely used by not-for-profits) are a good way of breaking through their media "clutter." Boomers prefer face-to-face and phone conversations.

The telephone is still neglected by far too many fund raisers. Roger Craver, writing in *Fund Raising Management*, asserts that "use of the telephone is particularly helpful for upgrading donors on your house file, for welcoming and upgrading new donors to your organization, for alerting donors to special needs and emergencies, for thanking donors, and for basic research into the needs and interests of individual donors." Baby Boomers are a key target audience; older individuals tend not to make phone gifts.

Fund raisers—and their trustees—often hesitate to use the telephone for fear that it will be viewed as invasive. And, although many people insist they hate telephone solicitations—up to 60% of consumers say they won't listen to an unsolicited sales pitch on the telephone—it works. As Ken Burnett, writing in *Relationship Fundraising*, reminds us so eloquently: **How many people get out of the bathtub to answer a letter?**

Thousands of combination direct mail and telephone programs have been used throughout the United States, Canada, and Europe by charities. This methodology is *telecommunications,* where success is measured by how many successful closings are accomplished, as opposed to *telemarketing,* where success is measured by how many contacts can be made in a defined period of time.

While the process works best when the prospective donor has a known relationship with the soliciting organization—an alumnus of a school, a former patient, a relative of a member of a religious order, a "family" member in some other identifiable way—acquisition programs based on lists with similar demographics to current members (age, postal code, income, educational level, even the magazines they read) have proved effective. It is most effective when used for moving "family" members to first-time contributors, restarting lapsed donors, and upgrading current contributors.

Much of the concerns can be eliminated by preceding the phone call with a pre-approach letter, explaining who will be called, why the call is being made, and when to expect it. Great care should be taken in both designing and processing the letters. Typically, they are individually addressed and word processed. Often, they are "live" signed or with a signature machine, hand-stamped, and sent via first class mail. Every component looks like a personal solicitation to the greatest possible degree: no indicia, no mass printed letter, no metered mail, no third class stamp. This is part of the cultivation process, designed to send the message: "We treat you as an individual."

After the pre-approach mailing, the phone call is placed by a trained caller. The call is used for fulfillment and bonding. It is a dialogue centered around a series of questions that cannot easily be answered with a yes or a no. "How do you feel about the needs that were presented by Mr. X in his letter to you?" "How do you feel about the suggested level of giving Ms. X has proposed?" The prospect, approached in this way, has the opportunity to have a conversation with the caller—the essence of face-to-face solicitation. Because combination direct mail and telephone programs follow the steps of the face-to-face solicitation process, potential donors receive two significant messages:

1. Their commitment is important to the organization both in terms of participation and size.

2. The organization views their commitment seriously and is willing to take time to finalize the pledge, even if that takes a series of cultivation/solicitation steps.

How well do combination direct mail and telephone programs work? Organizations report higher pledges and pledge rates than those using only traditional letter or phone call direct response programs. Although the focus of these programs are the lower-end donor, participating organizations have reported major gifts ranging from million-dollar bequests to outright gifts of ten thousand dollars and greater. Fulfillment rates are generally high, sometimes over 90%. For most organizations, the cost of the combination program is under 30 cents per dollar pledged, making it a very cost-effective vehicle.

Using the Internet (Young Adults)

Because younger audiences prefer it, an increased use of electronic newsletters, videos, e-mail and computer bulletin boards should be in your organization's future. Baby Busters and the Baby Boomlet are our first audiences who grew up with computerization. They expect to use the computer for their own philanthropy. Computer programs now allow people to look at information, interact (for example, by taking a brief quiz), and send for information on charities that interest them.

The Chronicle of Philanthropy reported on the Internet NonProfit Center, run entirely by volunteers. The Center was set up by buster Cliff Landesman, a graduate student at Princeton University in order to make it "faster, cheaper, and easier" for donors to learn about charities. Using the Center, you can peruse the "Best Buys for Big Hearts" list of the top charities in various categories, such as the environment or at- risk youth, as ranked by the American Institute of Philanthropy, a watchdog organization based in St. Louis. The institute bases its ranking on the percentage of a group's income that goes to charitable programs. You can also retrieve a "donor's Defense Kit" that includes tips on "how to say

Marketing on the Internet is different from other media

- You can't talk at the user but must, rather, talk with the user. Interact with the user whenever possible. Involve them in the marketing message and allow them the illusion of control.
- Make your message interesting. Educate and entertain the user with lively copy and graphics when appropriate. Change portions of the marketing message frequently to keep your presence fresh and inviting.
- Support and promote your commercial Internet presence. Index your location in Internet directories and use traditional communications and public relations practices to inform the public of your offline location.
- You must make information available with a means for response.

SOURCE: "The Basics of Marketing on the Internet," Jay Christensen, *DM News,* October 10, 1994.

'No' without guilt," electronic versions of charity annual reports, and suggestions about how to obtain more information on charities.

Other "roadmaps" are springing up to help potential donors navigate the Internet:

■ ReliefNet is a new network that provides information on international relief efforts, offers users a way to make a pledge electronically to the group(s) of their choice, and serves as a link to other information about relief efforts posted on the Internet. Jack Hidary, director of EarthWeb and creator of the ReliefNet, notes that most donors to relief groups tend to be over 40. "ReliefNet is a means of conveying to another generation the work that's being done."

The key to the future is delivering the information and accepting gift fulfillment in *whatever* format your donors prefer.

14 Legacy and Life Income Gift Opportunities

Accumulating savings and managing money will be major preoccupations for most maturing individuals in the years ahead. Living longer brings concerns about living well.

For that reason, many not-for-profits will find that, increasingly, major gifts will not be made as current gifts but rather through the combination of current and deferred gifting we call planned giving.

Use Planned Giving as the Key to Unlocking Major Gift Commitments

Mature Individuals

As today's older individual outlives her or his three score and ten, many are beginning to look to charities to help them plan for the last third of their lives.

As more of us live longer, our concerns grow in two areas:

- How will I fund my retirement?
- How will I cover end-of-life medical expenses?

Our conclusion may well be:
Giving away assets during life rather than at death is foolish.

As a result, "ultimate" gifts—sacrificial gifts of assets during one's lifetime—will be made reluctantly, at best. Would *you* be willing to make a major gift in your 60s, knowing you had another 20, 30 or more years of living?

SOURCE: *Pinpointing Affluence: Increasing Your Share of Major Donor Dollars*, Judith E. Nichols, Precept Press 1994.

■ **Older individuals are more concerned than mid-life individuals with the *management* of money.** "For this reason," notes Jeff Ostroff, author of *Successful Marketing to the 50+ Consumer*, "many older adults are likely to need the services of those who can help them oversee their assets, pay their bills, and protect their estates."

■ **They're spending their children's inheritances.** Today's mature individuals are more likely to be interested in life income vehicles that enhance a comfortable retirement than a financial planning vehicle which saves inheritance taxes.

To market planned giving successfully to mature individuals, remember they want to deal with people and organizations they can trust. Be sure to market positively! Don't describe negative "what if" scenarios. Aging is viewed positively by many affluent older individuals; treat them with dignity.

■ **Recognize that they hold more conservative attitudes towards money.** Mature individuals select financial vehicles with guaranteed safe investments, a high rate of return, and convenience as their priorities. Plagued by memories of bank failures, they often keep their assets in several institutions rather than consolidating them.

■ **Help them be more effective consumers.** Offer financial seminars free of charge. Be sure to schedule such offerings in the daytime. Many older persons dislike driving at night because of vision problems.

■ **Help them guard the nest.** Often, older individuals have been widowed or divorced. They may be contemplating remarriage or have a "signficant other." Romance at later ages brings with it concerns for protecting assets: both for the new partner and the family. Sensitive financial planning advice may be welcomed.

■ **Seek out the older newcomers to your community.** More affluent individuals are the most likely to "migrate" on retiring to cities and towns that provide cultural, educational and recreational opportunities.

Baby Boomers

Boomers view themselves as being "the best, the brightest"—they've been told this by their parents and the world in general since the day they were born. The assumptions which Boomers have internalized cause a dilemma: their view of themselves positions Boomers to be philanthropists and generous donors, yet their need for control makes them reluctant to "let go of dollars" even when they have major resources. (In fact, Boomers tend to choose payment plans and minimum payment vehicles even when these are not necessities.)

■ **Boomers use credit lines as earlier generations used savings accounts.** Knowing money keeps losing value, they are reluctant to actually part with it. In a sense, planned giving provides Boomer donors with a way to "have your cake and eat it too."

■ **Boomers have grown up in a world where sophisticated financial planning is a mark of status.** Magazines such as *Money* owe their rapid growth to Boomers' fascination with financial planning. At a younger age than more traditional prospects, Boomers are receptive to considering life insurance, stock gifts, and other personal property transfers, as well as the use of life-income vehicles, such as insurance, trusts, and annuities.

■ **Boomers may be entering a new financial stage of life: shifting from consumption and the present to savings and the future.** The combination of the resisted signs of aging coupled with their child-bearing have moved Boomers from conspicuous consumption to a somewhat more cautious stance. And, according to Jeff Ostroff, Boomers are more informed about the need to plan for retirement early: "They'll know, for example, that retirement could last 30 years or more."

Innovative marketing is the key to capturing a Boomer's interest in making a planned gift. Fund raisers need to sell the results, not the vehicle.

You cannot focus on the mechanisms of a trust or annuity; rather you must define the benefits in terms of Boomers' key needs:

- Financing their retirements
- Financing children's educations
- Financing their parents' aging

The last need—financing parents' aging—is an especially lucrative niche. If you inherit money in your 20s and 30s, it is used to further education, buy a first home, begin a business. But what if you inherit in your 50s or 60s? Chances are you've already made your major life moves and, in fact, these are your own highest income years. Inheritance may simply add to a tax burden.

Given this scenario, perhaps it's understandable that the results of a Mintel survey reported in *The Times* of London noted that eight out of 10 adults, especially the over-40s, really don't want to inherit anything. They would rather their parents spent it on having a cheerful old age.

Don't save up, mum—go on that cruise

"Look, Mum—spend it—turn the house into income—hock it—dump the Telecom shares—have the holiday, the sheltered flat, the ritzy nursing home, or at least the new toaster that doesn't spit sparks. We really don't want an inheritance. Spend it!"

SOURCE: Libby Purves' column, *The Times*, July 6, 1994.

A properly executed bequest and planned gift gives donors a bit of immortality. Psychologically, Boomers see themselves as major givers but often lack the immediate resources to make significant current gifts. Planned giving creates a bridge between their desires and reality.

WOMEN

Are you marketing your planned-giving program heavily to women? You should. After all:

Women outlive men. As a result women control the disposition of their own estates and, often, that of spouses and parents as well.

Women are increasingly not marrying and are taking responsibility for their own retirements and estate planning.

Women are becoming more affluent. More women are starting businesses and succeeding in middle and upper management. And, because women tend to save more than men, they are accumulating more assets.

■ **To reach women, be sensitive.** Don't treat women like men. Too often, financial planning advice is delivered patronizingly. Educate your financial advisors.

■ **Women prefer a soft-sell, relationship-building approach.** They tend to be more financially conservative than men, often favoring less risky financial vehicles and looking for demonstrated fiscal accountability.

■ **Market to women earlier.** Women are ready for financial planning at earlier and earlier ages. Begin your cultivation with appeals to women in their mid-40s. Increasing numbers of more affluent women are remaining single by choice or lack of it or become single at mid-life through divorce or widowhood.

■ **Provide women with resources.** Hold seminars and workshops on financial planning. Focus a segment on issues of concern for women.

Send a newsletter to female prospects focusing on retirement planning from their perspective.

■ **Visit women.** Try to see all the women on your prospect list. Take a few months and see only women. You'll be surprised at how much you've been concentrating on male prospects. Follow up with all referrals of women even if, on the surface, they don't appear to be good prospects. Women have not been cultivated, by and large, and are often overlooked by the largely male financial planning community.

■ **Solve elder care problems.** Many Boomer and World War II women are now assisting aging parents. Many will spend more time providing elder care than child care. The "sandwiched generation" needs help in planning ahead.

■ **Recognize that many women shun publicity and recognition.** They often prefer to honor others through their giving. The opportunity to pay tribute to a parent or other loved one is more likely to trigger a gift than a chance for personal recognition.

■ **Be patient.** Recognize that many women are more concerned with their ability to replace gifts of wealth. Their first use of a life income vehicle will probably be modest.

Planned giving is the necessary complement to your annual and major giving programs. As people live longer, bequests and estate giving will be increasingly accepted as the logical extension of current giving. Begin preparing now.

15 Attracting Trustees and Volunteers

The changing demographics will affect more than simply who your donors and prospects are and how you'll reach them. There will also be a serious impact on volunteers—those unpaid, well-educated trustees, campaign leaders, key fund-raising volunteers, and other volunteers whose generous donations of time are among the most important gifts your organization receives.

According to a study done by the Charities Aid Foundation in London, volunteerism is highest in Spain (with 71% of the population volunteering) and lowest in France (27%). Great Britain (65%), Canada (62%) and the U.S.A. (55%) rely heavily on volunteer resources. In Canada, volunteers tend to give over five hours a month, while for the other nations it averages out to between about an hour and a half (1.6 for both France and Spain) to around two hours monthly (1.8 for the United Kingdom and 2.2 in the United States).

It's a Seller's Market

Volunteers are still available, but you must understand that we've entered a "seller's market." More and more charitable causes are competing for the best of the volunteer pool, a pool that is both changing and shrinking. Whereas the volunteer of the past shared a common background with other volunteers—and with your staff—today's volunteer may not.

■ **Flexibility will be the key to attracting and keeping volunteers.** Compared to the volunteers you've been used to working with, today's and tomorrow's volunteers will be less willing (and probably

Flexibility: The Key to Happy Volunteers

Marshall Sewell Jr., a now-retired fund raising executive, described for Fund Raising Management *magazine what is certain to become an increasingly familiar situation:*

When Burt Allen walked into our hospital development office, we knew he would be an ideal fund-raising volunteer. A retired Army general, congenial, friendly, intelligent, and persuasive, he understood immediately what we were doing and he appeared to have empathy with the people he would be contacting.

But he had one condition before saying yes: "If I'm supposed to work on Tuesday, and Tuesday turns out to be a good golfing day, can I come in on Wednesday?"

I said, "You've got a deal."

Our hospital volunteer coordinator objected. It won't work, she said.

I understood her viewpoint. When you're staffing a nursing station or scheduling couriers to carry blood samples to your laboratory, you've got to know that your volunteer is coming in that day. But is development such a life-or-death matter?

Now that I'm retired, I realize how much retirees appreciate their freedom from bosses and rigid schedules, so why not encourage more flexibility when recruiting volunteers?

less able) to accept the rigidity we've traditionally built into our volunteer programs.

Mr. Sewell saw it accurately: flexibility will be the key to attracting the best fund-raising volunteers of the future, and not just the older ones. *Time has become our most precious commodity.*

■ **Make volunteering a positive experience.** Your new volunteers need to believe that working with your organization makes sense for them. You'll need to provide them with interesting "job opportunities" that meet their needs for companionship, skill training, and networking. You'll have to provide your volunteers with attractive options—options that fit their lifestyles, their cultural backgrounds, their emotional needs, and their ideas about what personal benefits they will achieve as a volunteer to your organization.

■ **Saying thank you—loudly, often, and meaningfully—is a must.** Showing appreciation is always the right thing to do. In today's competitive volunteer market, it's a must. You need to find ways of saying thank you that are especially meaningful to each of the demographic and psychographic cohorts you are trying to attract as volunteers.

You'll need to formalize your volunteer appreciation program: thank volunteers in print, thank them publicly, thank them in their own trade publications, have your CEO or president thank them personally. Use certificates and special events. Acknowledge goals that are met and other accomplishments.

Volunteering is "In"

Whereas the charitable of the '80s wanted to be photographed making the scene at black-tie galas, the '90s ideal is to spend one's spare time helping out at a soup kitchen, tutoring ghetto teenagers, or bedsitting someone with AIDS. Check writing is now considered ersatz, a salve to the bourgeois conscience. Under the new code, involvement alone is deemed worthwhile, either for givers or the recipients of assistance.

SOURCE: *Worth Magazine,* Oct./Nov. 1992 issue, quoted in the *Chronicle of Philanthropy,* Oct. 20, 1992.

By addressing the three keys of flexibility, self-interest, and appreciation, you'll be able to tap new sources of volunteer help. Very likely, these sources have been untapped or under-utilized by your organizaton. But be aware that addressing the needs of your emerging volunteer pool takes work on your part—research and a budget.

Attracting Mature Individuals as Volunteers

It's not difficult to recruit mature individuals as volunteers. As "Civics" and "Adaptives," many older individuals have grown up with a long tradition of philanthropy. As former U.S. President George Bush noted: "We must bring in the generations, harnessing the unused talent of the elderly...For not only leadership is passed from generation to generation, but so is stewardship."

But you've got to be sensitive to older individuals' needs and feelings. For example, contrary to how most younger people think, mature individuals don't see themselves as having "all the time in the world." Instead, they may see themselves as having a limited number of good years left and will be careful about how they use their time. They don't plan to spend their retirement years before the television. They travel, exercise, and seek out new learning experiences. It's your job to provide these experiences as part of your volunteer program.

■ **Recruit them through friends and peers.** Older adults tend to cluster. You'll find them attending "every Wednesday" groups at community centers, at service club luncheons, at low-cost or free daytime programs offered through universities and arts organizations, and at activities that emphasize their interests, including financial workshops.

■ **Make them a part of your group.** Keep them posted on your fundraising goals and activities. Welcome them every time they enter your premises. Cut them in on the campaign gossip.

■ **Let them do something different if they want to.** Let older volunteers pick their own jobs. The retired corporate CEO may, in fact, want to continue as campaign chair. Or she may have had enough of leadership in any form. The former accountant might prefer to edit the newsletter. The doctor might prefer the opportunity to organize the mailroom.

■ **Watch out for sensitivities.** If younger volunteers feel ignored or insulted, they'll probably just move on to another organization. But older volunteers often drop out entirely. The work they do for your organization may represent a major portion of their lives.

Volunteering Adds Longevity

Giving time to charitable causes may play a key role in living longer, healthier lives. Researchers tracking 300 women found that those who had been members of a club or volunteered with an organization were less likely to have suffered major illness over a 30-year period and tended to live longer.

SOURCE: Study by Phyllis Moen, Cornell University, June 1992.

■ **Recognize service milestones.** Older volunteers are apt to give more time than younger ones. They appreciate that commitment being acknowledged regularly with certificates, service pins, a luncheon of appreciation.

■ **Cover their costs.** Many older volunteers are on fixed incomes and worry about the small costs adding up. Give them free parking, reimburse their travel expenses promptly, provide meals and snacks. Don't let them spend a cent on being a volunteer but always give them the opportunity to make a charitable donation.

■ **Watch your physical facilities.** There are some physical limitations to growing older. Put volunteer offices on the first floor if there isn't an elevator; reserve parking spots in front of the building; make your premises welcoming with bright lighting and oversized signs.

■ **Let them serve as part-time consultants.** Many mature people don't want to retire fully. If older individuals have skills you can use on an ongoing basis, consider paying them as consultants. Their expertise—accounting, legal, etc.—may be available for a truly modest fee.

Attracting Baby Boomers as Volunteers

Contributing to the public good is a high priority for Baby Boomers. As "idealists," they are positioned to see volunteering as part of their value system.

To attract Boomers you must offer assignments that reinforce their sense of being special. Boomers look for opportunities to demonstrate their skills, expertise, and competence. They won't be interested in what they see as "routine" work. Boomers also tend to be more interested in volunteer assignments that help them make contacts with people who might be useful to know: business contacts or social contacts. While this is not a new rationale for volunteering, with Boomers it tends to be a stronger motivation than for mature audiences.

Just like Marshall Sewell's retired general, Boomers need flexibility. Many have married relatively late in life: they're juggling job and family responsibilities. Many are members of time-pressed, two-career families with young children.

Boomers are not difficult to identify and recruit. In addition to having idealistic personalities, they've grown up in competition with others of their generation. So they tend to look for ways to promote themselves. Boomers thrive on publicity. Signficiant fund raising generates lots of notice. If Boomers see your fund-raising program as being potentially useful in bringing them visibility, they will seek you out.

■ **Making volunteering useful.** Provide networking opportunities that work for Boomers—professionally or personally. Introduce Boomer volunteers to trustees. Provide them with access to top staff people. Arrange for Boomers to mingle with other volunteers.

■ **Provide instant and unique gratification.** Send an immediate letter of appreciation to your new special gifts volunteer with a copy to her or his employer. List the names of the campaign committee prominently in your annual report and newsletter. Display their names in your lobby on a "welcoming board." Give them a name plate and badge.

■ **Make your working conditions attractive.** Are your hours convenient? Boomers like to meet early in the morning or right after work. Do you provide child care for weekend or evening meetings? Is there a physical place your volunteer can call her or his own? Let them personalize it with plants and graphics. Can they get food and drink that fits their lifestyles? Herbal teas, custom coffees, fruit juices, yogurt, and mineral water are Boomer snacks of choice.

■ **Ask them to participate in designing their own volunteer jobs.** Boomers see themselves as professionals. Respect their expertise.

■ **Offer short-term volunteer activities.** Because of their time-pressed lives, many Boomers hesitate to commit to long-term volunteering. Consider assignments for just hours, a day, or a week.

Attracting Women as Volunteers

Volunteer work is part of women's tradition. In most societies, women have played a greater role than men in volunteering for social and charitable causes. But many nonprofit causes are so busy trying to find the traditional homemaker available to lick stamps and stuff envelopes from 9:00am to 3:00pm five days a week, that they have missed a growing volunteer pool: the capable, well-educated, busy, working woman.

As an increasing proportion of the female population moves into the workforce, the female volunteer is changing. She is more likely to be a busy executive who, like her male counterpart, wants to give something back to her community in return for some defined personal goals. To do this, she may well have to buck a situation in which she is ignored for leadership roles or where a few token women are "recycled" from one fund-raising leadership post to another.

■ **Search where talented women abound.** Nonprofit causes need to be proactive in identifying and recruiting women. Introduce your organization and yourself to women by attending professional women's groups. Sit with women at mixed-sex professional luncheons. Look in professional publications, business journals, and alumnae magazines for promotions and news items: write notes of congratulation and mention that you're searching for talented volunteers.

■ **Be free of stereotyping.** Treat women volunteers as capable equals. Give them assignments with visibility and responsibility.

Don't restrict them to the "soft" campaign assignments. Avoid asking them to take minutes at the committee meeting. Never assume they will make the coffee.

■ **Don't isolate them.** Women, just like men, are looking for contacts. Be sure they are plugged into the network of social and business events.

■ **Offer child care to everyone.** Because of changing demographics, today's woman is juggling multiple responsibilities, not the least of which may be children. Woman are often reluctant to bring up the need for child care. Decide on a child care policy for all volunteers. If you decide to offer child care on site or will pay for babysitting, communicate this—as part of your volunteer recruitment process—to potential volunteers. The cost to your organization will be modest compared to the quality efforts resulting from a first-class volunteer.

■ **Be alert to safety.** It's not chauvinistic to be concerned for a woman's safety. Even CEOs shouldn't be expected to leave the building unescorted at night. Unlocked doors, poor lighting, and lack of patrols can contribute to unpleasant (or worse) situations. Again, many women are reluctant to bring up concerns. It's your job to anticipate and diffuse potential negatives.

Attracting Baby Busters as Volunteers

Younger adults have an extremely high record of volunteerism. However we have a tendency to ignore their contributions. Busters tend to "personalize" their philanthropy. They give where they volunteer.

■ **Catch their attention by using peers and appropriate vehicles.** Even more so than to their older brothers and sisters, Busters believe in the importance of friends and family. Use spokespersons from their own generation.

■ **Give them a specific role to play.** Post-Boomers are not trying to change things. They want to fix things. Active projects—planting trees, cleaning up beaches, painting lower-income houses—are very attractive to them.

■ **Keep in mind that teens, probably more than any other consumer group, desire immediate gratification.** You may want to tie appreciation tokens to small increments of volunteerism.

■ **Post information at their schools and gathering places.** The vast majority of Busters are still in school. Consider holding a volunteer fair—in conjunction with other charitable organizations—on campus.

■ **Use cyberspace.** Post volunteer job opportunities on electronic community bulletin boards. Or place an inquiry on the appropriate special-interest electronic forums on the Internet.

■ **Use the right media.** Get public service announcements played on radio stations that target those in their teens and early 20s. Seek out the newspapers (including college publications) for articles and interviews.

Attracting a Diverse Group of Volunteers

Cultural differences can make recruitment of individuals with backgrounds other than that predominating at an organization difficult. The key is to know what the differences are. In some cultures, it's best to recruit men first. Or, to invite the community as a group to consider volunteerism.

■ **Give back before you ask.** Be sure your organization has been proactive in serving the community. Sometimes communication is poor between a "traditional" nonprofit and a newly-emerging population group. A meeting with community leaders may help to clarify how your organization is perceived.

■ **Recruit visibly and actively.** Recruit in the neighborhood using local publications and media. Don't be guilty of "recycling" the few, highly visible members of a community.

■ **Make your cause look friendly and familiar.** Does your staffing reflect the diversity you're trying to attract in volunteers? Do your printed materials (including office photographs and pictures) demonstrate that you are inclusive? Does the music you play in the waiting area include melodies familiar to a variety of cultures?

Above all, remember that for many of our future volunteers—just as with those volunteers who served in the past and do so now—the primary motivation is to give back to their communities. Make volunteering a positive experience so that they can feel good about meeting their obligation.

16

Emerging Trends in Corporate, Trust and Foundation Relations

Make Corporate Support a Win-Win Partnership

Originally, corporate philanthropy was a voluntary response to social issues and problems. Over the centuries it evolved into mandated corporate involvement. Increasingly now, corporate philanthropy appears to be evolving into a phase in which social responsibility is viewed as an investment by corporations.

Most of our ideas of corporate philanthropy are a carryover from the industrial era, which effectively ended in the late 1980s. In the old paradigm, it was paramount that corporate philanthropy initiatives be pure in motive. In the new view, mixed motives serve the public interest just fine, so long as they produce good results. According to the new paradigm, society is well-served when corporations, governments, and nonprofits synergistically serve the interests of each section. The fastest-growing ties between nonprofits and companies are business-to-business relationships. The key is to draw on the resources of several different budgets within the donor company.

Strategic philanthropy has entered the corporate lexicon. More than ever before, organizations are targeting their giving to enhance their corporate goals and missions. Enlightened self-interest—benefiting both the company and society—goes beyond outright grants. It includes "people-giving"—making employees at all levels available for work, sometimes on company time.

Understanding Marketing-Driven Philanthropy

While the outright charitable budget is often being cut at corporations, profit-motivated philanthropy (often called cause-related marketing—a term copyrighted by the Travel-Related Services United of the American Express Company) is the area of growth for larger companies and, increasingly, for small businesses as well.

That's because companies want—and need—to reach the lucrative but segmented constituencies of Boomers, mature individuals, Busters and Boomlets, as well as women and ethnically and culturally diverse populations. But often, the experiences of these target consumers has left them doubting the companies courting them. In a society which no longer trusts businesses nor government, nonprofits and charities still have credibility. The desire on the part of the business to align itself with well-regarded partners is behind the surge of sponsorships and other partnerships between business and not-for-profits.

Because cause-related marketing is a versatile tool, it can be used to realize a broad range of organizational and marketing objectives. For example:

- gaining national visibility
- enhancing corporate image
- thwarting negative publicity
- pacifying customer groups
- increasing brand awareness
- increasing brand recognition
- enhancing brand image

- broadening customer base
- reaching new market segments and geographic markets

With receptive business leadership encouraging not-for-profits to bring ideas to it, the profit-motivated giving pocket of corporate philanthropy and marketing is clearly going to continue to grow. Both companies and nonprofits are, generally, pleased with their experiences and plan to continue their activities. Both sides expect to see more for-profit support of special events such as concerts, walkathons, and sports tournaments. Alcohol, tobacco, and pharmaceutical companies, for example, which may feel that direct-purchase incentives (such as coupon redemptions) are inappropriate for their products, find sponsorships ideal.

A key to attracting market-driven philanthropy is to "know yourself." Not-for-profits whose constituencies mirror key demographic targets need to provide potential corporate partners with clear examples of the match: how their organization is perceived positively by the demographic group(s) and how support will benefit both partners. Warner Canto, vice president of special projects for American Express, rightfully decries the many cause-marketing programs that have been "poorly conceived," featuring "inappropriate causes" and "ill-defined objectives." He urges businesses to apply the same marketing disciplines to cause-marketing programs as they do to other marketing efforts, and he calls for nonprofits to become better marketers.

Profit-motivated philanthropy is at its most complex when addressed to Boomers. Increasingly, Boomers are occupying the seats of leadership in the very corporations seeking to attract them as customers and consumers. Cause-related marketing which mirrors how Boomers see themselves is accepted, even enthusiastically welcomed.

■ Cause-related marketing combines traditional and nontraditional values well:

> Bob Geldoff, the Irish rock musician, whose Band Aid raised US $110 million (UK £75 million) for the relief of African famine, demonstrates how responsive Boomers will be when touched properly. Combining Boomer values of globalism and family with their love of music and the assurance that "every penny you give goes to the cause" proved to be the key in motivating

> a constituency most had ignored. Michael Norton, who heads London's Directory of Social Change, suggests that Band Aid "didn't need to raise money. The news media, especially TV, raised it for them. Band Aid just needed to provide a channel for the money to flow in."

- Cause-related marketing appeals to Boomers' fondness for the 1950s and 1960s:

> Seeking to update its image, Wisk—an American detergent—joined forces with local festivals, fairs, and special events to provide a 24-minute fireworks display which concluded wth a special "ring around the sky," symbolizing the famous Wisk "Ring around the Collar" ad theme. The fireworks were choreographed to the music of 30 years of rock and roll.

- Some approaches to Boomers focus on life stages:

> Masco, a major U.S. corporation with subsidiaries in home furnishings, noted in its annual report that it was "Targeting the Future . . ." and suggested it was sure to do well because of Baby Boomers, both because they were better educated and at the peak of their earnings capacity and because of the Boomers' "cocooning" phenomenon.

For companies like Masco, who sell home-related products or services, there is logic in sponsoring quality public television broadcasting—at-home upscale entertainment. Suggest to potential partners they can address Boomers' fitness needs by funding medical research on back pain and furniture at a school of medicine. Or, working with Boomer concerns by providing furniture for a day or elder care center.

Older individuals are not being ignored by companies seeking cause-related ventures. Masters and senior tournaments of golf and tennis are on the upswing. Opportunities await the company that partners with a not-for-profit that can reach subsegments within the mature market.

> I talked with a marketing representative from McDonald's, possibly the most demographically-aware corporation. Their commercials now segment out older individuals both as consumers and as employees. I asked if there were any plans for a Ronald McDonald House for the spouses and families of the elderly dealing with catastrophic illness. While no specifics have been agreed upon, she indicated that McDonald's was looking for projects along that line.

Marrying art and culture with customer outreach is fairly common in cause-related marketing. Art and music may be the best bridge for reaching culturally diverse populations.

In the United States, for example, many cause-related projects have targeted improving relationships with the Hispanic community—the U.S.A.'s fastest-growing ethnic population.

> McDonald's sponsored the Hispanic Heritage Art contest in the mid-1980s. Brochures promoting the contest were distributed to bilingual education teachers in Hispanic communities throughout the United States. The Capitol Children's Museum in Washington, D.C., displayed the prize-winning entries, and grand-prize winners presented their drawings to the President of the United States during Hispanic Heritage Week.

> More recently, Coors Beer sponsored a two-year tour of Hispanic art. Pepsi-Cola and Coca-Cola both have sponsored Hispanic music awards, and Pepsi features Miami Sound Machine, a well-known Hispanic group, in its commercials.

> Among the recent projects sponsored by the AT&T Foundation is a traveling exhibit of Hispanic art, the first major exhibit of Hispanic work to go into mainstream museums. The support was given for "good reasons," but there is "no denying the Hispanic population is important in the marketplace," says Timothy McClimon, who adds that AT&T has professionals dedicated solely to marketing to that group.

> Similarly, Philip Morris Companies Inc. has sponsored "The Latin American Spirit: Art and Artists in the United States, 1920-1970." The tour moved from the Bronx, New York, to El Paso, Texas, to San Diego, California, to San Juan, Puerto Rico, to Vero Beach, Florida—all major concentrations for Hispanic Americans. Why is Philip Morris doing this? Possibly because Hispanic Americans are the youngest of target groups, prime potential consumers of tobacco products.

Similar sponsorship opportunities can be created for any segment of a country's population that companies need to reach.

Women's more personal focus has identified different cause-marketing directions. Johnson & Johnson wanted to create a group promotion event that would have maximum consumer "pull" with women—the key consumers for J&J products. To target Boomer women, a campaign focusing on the issue of domestic violence was created. Called "Shelter Aid," the program combined an outright donation from J&J to establish and operate a toll-free domestic-violence hotline with consumer involvement via coupon redemption and point-of-purchase donation canisters. The program featured an extensive public relations program featuring actress Lindsay Wagner.

Cause-related marketing can be psychographically driven. Sometimes, corporations and businesses are better served by defining potential consumers in terms of shared similar attitudes. Rather than demographics, psychographics are the key to choosing a not-for-profit partner. Businesses look for not-for-profit organizations which can suggest projects to which groups of dissimilar individuals might react to in a like fashion.

> MasterCard, for example, encouraged its U.S. cardholders to be involved in the allocation of funds among several charities using a balloting process. "Choose to Make a Difference" benefitted the Alzheimer's Association, American Cancer Society, American Heart Association, American Red Cross, Just Say No Foundation, and the National Committee for Prevention of Child Abuse. MasterCard

> hoped to enhance its image (and increase card usage!) with those individuals most likely to respond positively to being involved in directing MasterCard's charitable giving. Concerns about stewardship are typical of a wide demographic grouping of affluent individuals—key users of credit cards.
>
> Similarly, Spiegel, Inc., has used cause-related marketing to increase catalog sales. Spiegel donates 33 cents from each order it receives from a "Holiday Thrills" gift collection catalog marketed at Christmas.

Environmental concerns may be the "hot" cause-related marketing issue for the future. In the 1970s and '80s, Boomers ushered in "the Green Revolution." We may well be approaching the Aware Decade, when "every purchase made by family and by business will be influenced not just by price, convenience and profit, but by the product's effect on life on earth," asserts writer Joel Makower.

Environmental protection is emerging as a "consensus issue." According to a Gallup Report, "Concern about ecological issues is no longer associated primarily with younger, better-educated people who were in the vanguard of the environmental movement two decades ago. Today, environmentalists comprise a broad-based coalition from diverse social and economic backgrounds."

Already, partnerships are being formed. American television shows are speaking out on environmental issues, due in part to meetings between the show's writers and the Environmental Media Association. And, interviewed on the eve on his 1990 World Tour, Paul McCartney emerged as an environmental spokesman and guardian of the ecology: "Linda and I decided we could go out, have fun entertaining the fans and make a bit of money," he says. "Or we could do all that and something worthwhile at the same time. Environmental concerns were a logical choice for us."

Cause-related marketing partnerships can be a golden opportunity for both partners. Guidelines for cause-related marketing have been developed by the Council of the Better Business Bureau's Philanthropic Advisory Service in the United States. Here are nine suggestions for businesses and charities considering participation in joint-venture marketing:

1. Is the charity familiar with the participating corporation's subsidiaries, products and/or services?

2. Is the corporation informed about the participating charity's programs, finances, and other fund-raising efforts?

3. Is there a written agreement that gives formal permission for the corporation to use the charity's name and logo?

4. Does the written agreement: (a) give the charity prior review and approval of ad materials that use its name, (b) indicate how long the campaign will last, (c) specifiy how and when charitable funds will be distributed, (d) explain any steps that will be taken in case of a disagreement or unforeseen result with the promotion?

5. Do the joint-venture advertisements: (a) specify the actual or anticipated portion of the sales or service price to benefit the charity, (b) indicate the full name of the charity, (c) include an address or phone number to contact for additional information about the charity or the campaign, (d) indicate when the campaign will end and, if applicable, the maximum amount the charity will receive?

6. Does the promotion follow all applicable government regulations in the areas the marketing will take place?*

7. Does the corporation have fiscal controls in place to process and record the monies received to benefit the charity?

8. Will more than one charity be involved in the promotion? If so, how will funds be distributed?

9. Will the corporation complete a financial report at the end of the campaign (or annually, if the campaign lasts more than a year), which identifies (a) the total amount collected for the charity, (b) any campaign expenses, and (c) how much the charity received?

---

*In the United Kingdom, the recent Charities Act legislates the way companies act in such joint ventures.

Targeting Emerging Businesses

Sometimes your best "corporate" prospect isn't a large company but a small business. Whether you're searching for an annual contribution, a special gift, sponsorship, underwriting, or volunteer help, don't ignore those with less than 100 employees. Under 100 companies are the fastest-growing business segment of our societies. The trend is demographically driven:

■ **Baby Boomers are enthusiastic entrepreneurs.** Leon Danco, president of the Center for Family Business, an educational and consulting firm in the U.S., asserts that members of this generation are "clearly entrepreneurially inclined, excited by the romance of going into business for themselves." Boomer interest in owning their own companies has fueled the growth of magazines such as *Inc.* and *Home Business.*

Boomers value entrepreneurship over climbing the corporate career ladder. The Boomer hero is epitomized in Steve Jobs, the cofounder of Apple Computers, who made a fortune with personal computers and then was forced to resign when he made moves to start a whole new enterprise, Next, Inc. "It's the idea that you can do it in the garage and wag your finger at IBM and get away with it," writes Landon Jones in *Great Expectations.* "And then when the company gets too institutionalized and oppressive, you start over."

Boomers look at smaller self-owned businesses as an alternative to the crowded path to the top of the corporate ladder. With competition so fierce for a limited number of key positions, many Boomers are opting out of the corporate competition in increasing numbers. "We have a lot less loyalty to companies, and we put up with a lot less than our parents," concedes Rich Garnitz, a Boomer who quit his job as a marketing manager at Xerox and started his own life-planning firm.

Family togetherness, a Boomer value, is a renewed priority. Combining work and lesiure whenever possible is a unqiue characteristic of Boomers. "Many couples are seeking ways to integrate their work life and their home life," notes Sharon Nelton, a family business expert at the U.S. Chamber of Commerce and the author of *In Love and Business*, a study of entrepreneurial couples.

Boomers Rebecca and Dan Matthias decided to run a business together even *before* they were married. "I think we discussed it on our first date," says Rebecca. By their second anniversary, she and Dan had launched Mothers Work Inc., a Philadelphia manufacturer and retailer of maternity clothes, which caters to today's working woman. The successful company has had its growth fueled by Boomer women demands.

■ **Older individuals are viewing retirement as a beginning, not an end.** It used to be that we were born, went to school, worked at a job, and then—if we were fortunate—enjoyed a few years of retirement before dying. No more. As life has lengthened, it is not unusual for mature individuals to return to school, start second families, and begin new career adventures. Increasing life expectancy and better health among older populations are altering the very definitions of "old age" and retirement. Mature individuals both need and want to work. They are attracted to the flexibility and challenge of starting their own businesses.

■ **Women are starting businesses in record numbers.** Today, women are better educated and more business-oriented than ever. The "glass ceiling," which stops many women from attaining higher ranks in corporations, causes many talented female executives to simply bypass the frustrations of corporate life by leaving the system and going into business for themselves.

For many women, entrepreneurship solves the problems of combining family responsibilities with a desire for higher income. The majority of today's female business owners have (or start out with) home-based operations—helped along by the technological advances and the increasing affordability of communication tools such as personal computers, mobile telephones, modems, and fax machines.

Marketing Keys for Corporate Support

■ **Propose a partnership that solves corporate employee needs.** David Bloom, Ph.D., professor of Economics at Columbia University, New York, and other economists see a general tightening of the labor market as the century draws to a close. This, they believe, will not only force employers to compete for the services of working mothers, but will encourage companies to attempt to lure non-working mothers into the market.

Provide help with child-care expertise. "Despite the rapid entry of women with young children into the work force, many mothers are still prevented from working by the scarcity and high cost of quality child care," Bloom says. He notes that "employers are beginning to see the link between daycare initiatives and bottom-line profitabilty. The stage is definitely set for child care to become *the* fringe benefit." Barbara Adolf, the author of *The Employer's Guide to Child Care*, concurs, reporting that "corporations are rethinking the relationship between work life and home life, recognizing that work and family can no longer be considered separate."

> The DuPont Corporation responded to the needs of its employees by renovating a facility for day care and then turning it over to the local YMCA whose expertise qualified it as the logical manager. The results: a win-win solution for employees, employer, and the YMCA.

Offer help with aging parents. Many Boomer women will spend more time carrying for aging parents than raising children. Ken Dychtwald, author of *AgeWave,* predicts that elder care, not child care, may be the true concern for employees in the coming century.

■ **Help build employee loyalty.** This is a true concern for corporations. Because Boomers have always been in competition given their greater numbers, they have tended to change jobs more frequently than previous generations.

Research has noted that corporate involvement in public service can help retain these valuable employees: workers surveyed say their loyalty increases if their corporations are involved in public service. A significant percentage (37%) say they would feel more loyal if they knew about the charitable contributions of their company. Other research has found that companies that exhibit social consciousness perform better financially when compared to companies that are less involved with social issues.

Reward employee volunteerism. "Some companies, such as Xerox and Wells Fargo, offer employees paid community-involvement sabbaticals, during which they can work with nonprofit agencies. At Xerox, employees can take up to a year at full pay and benefits; at Wells Fargo, they can take up to six months. As a result, a senior systems analyst at Wells Fargo took six months off to organize and promote recreational programs for disabled people; a project manager helped a child-abuse prevention program develop drop-in centers; and an assistant vice president developed a countrywide organ-donor awareness program," reports Ken Dychtwald.

Don't sell your organization's value short. "Many nonprofits are sitting on their own undervalued assets," says Alan Toman, president of Marketing Department, Inc., a New York-based firm that specializes in helping to bring corporations and nonprofits together in marketing arrangements. He is convinced that nonprofits can offer highly targeted, segmented ways to reach key population groups. As he says:

> Nonprofits know the market extremely well. Their participation gives the company the equivalent of a Good Housekeeping Seal of Approval.

New Directions for Foundation Giving

Private foundation giving is mirroring the concerns and interests of the post World War II donors now establishing these vehicles. While many of us tend to think of private foundations in terms of the giants—Ford, Carnegie, Rockefeller—the typical foundation or trust is much more modest: created by a living donor in 1959 with US $100,000 in assets, today has US $600,000 in assets, four trustees, and often includes the donor or family members on the board.

■ **Women are in the forefront of creating private foundations.** Although the overall rate of formation of both large and small foundations has declined since mid-century, Elizabeth Boris—political scientist and vice president for research at the Council of Foundations in Washington, DC—sees reason for optimism. Why? Because of women. As women begin to "take greater control of their wealth... foundations may continue to be vehicles to meet their charitable needs." Although women created only 20% of the foundations started before 1970, they were responsible for 48%—nearly half—of those foundations formed since 1970. Women's areas of philanthropic concern, however, are often very different from those of men. Their foundations often target child abuse, domestic violence, and environmental issues as priorities.

■ **Younger philanthropists are breaking away from the more traditional funding recipients of their families.** Boomer George S. Pillsbury, Jr., a member of Yale's Class of 1972, chose not to spend his baking company inheritance on his alma mater. Rather, George Junior's money goes to grassroots organizations fighting, among other things, toxic waste, apartheid in South Africa, and discrimination against lesbians and gays. This is a dramatic departure from his father's priorities, which center heavily around higher education.

Likewise, Chuck E. Collins, the great-grandson of Oscar Mayer and a 1983 graduate of Hampshire College, donated his entire $300,000 inheritance to disarmament groups, minority leadership projects, and a variety of grassroots organizations supporting liberal causes. And John W. Hicklooper, Jr., who inherited "in the six figures" on his 21st birthday in 1974, used his money to help start a progressive community fund, giving money to political theatre troupes, environmental groups fighting industrial pollution, and organizations for people who have been hurt through the farming crisis.

Under the leadership of such younger philanthropists, a number of new foundations are being established. The Funding Exchange Inc., a network of social-change foundations established in 1979 by Mr. Pillsbury and other like-minded wealthy heirs had 4,000 donors in 1988, contributing about US $5 million to 1,200 grassroots organizations.

The change in direction evidenced by these examples may be the "tip of the iceberg." Many of the social-change-oriented philanthropists are under 40. In the near future, many will sit on the boards of family foundations. They may well change the direction of these more traditional foundations. It is not unreasonable to suggest that the priorities of foundations and trusts in the 21st century will closely parallel the interests of Boomers.

A Response to Changing Leadership

Not only is it likely that the focus of private foundations and trusts will shift, but there is likely to be a change as well in how these funders view their participation. Not only will the funders be

Boomers: Increasingly, Boomers will also serve as the executive directors and staff at foundations.

The Ford Foundation's report, *The Common Good: Social Welfare and the American Future*, heralds a changing spirit likely to catch on worldwide. While continuing to endorse progressive solutions to problems, the foundation has changed its overall tone as reflected by its three guiding principles:

- Pragmatism: Popular support can be generated for programs that address obvious problems in a cost-effective way.
- Respect for the family: Government policy should strengthen the family rather than undermine it.
- Accountability: Social policy should offer protection as well as opportunity, but it ought not to offer protection in such a way that fosters dependency and closes off opportunity.

Both what will be supported and how foundations will view their role will differ from the approach taken by past leadership.

■ **More hands-on involvement.** There is less of a tendency to support established charities, and more interest in encouraging new directions. Many Boomers reject adding money to established vehicles, including scholarship funds and "traditional" vehicles, preferring to furnish seed money to encourage trial programs and projects that might not otherwise exist.

■ **A concern for relevance.** Even the more conservative private foundations are likely to find their priorities changing in order to remain relevant in the years ahead. Issues involving aging and elder care, poverty as it affects immigrants and diverse populations, as well as concerns about improving the environment and strengthening family life will increasingly be the proposals most likely to be funded.

■ **A concern for independence rather than dependence.** Increasingly funders will see themselves as "seeding" programs and encouraging pilot projects rather than furnishing ongoing operational support. Not-for-profits who demonstrate leadership by using their expertise to break new ground will find their organizations in the forefront to receive foundation grants for their work.

■ **A concern for accountability and stewardship.** Just as these concerns are increasing for individuals, accountability and stewardship will be top priorities for foundations and trusts as well. Even more so than in the past, appropriate reporting and demonstrated results will be expected by those who award grants.

As we enter the 21st century, successful marketing to and fund raising from companies and private trusts must parallel the efforts that work for attracting individual commitments. Not surprisingly we will find that, increasing, the case for support must address the needs of the potential funder. As not-for-profits become more comfortable with articulating their own demographic and psychographic profiles, companies and private trusts will respond with more and better partnership possibilities.

What's Hot and What's Not

Religious Giving: A Concern for *All* Fund Raisers

Because those who give generously to religion also tend to give generously to other charities, *all* fund raisers should be concerned about potential changes in the patterns of religious giving. According to research conducted by Yankelovich, Skelly, and White for the Rockefeller Brothers Fund, "if an individual is moved to make a contribution to religious causes/programs, then that same individual is more likely to support non-religious activities than someone who does not give to a church, synagogue, etc."

Religious beliefs/convictions motivate individuals to consider giving to the following (in rank order):

a) charities that assist the poor

b) organizations that help needy people in other countries
c) medical charities, and
d) educational institutions

The Good News

The Rockefeller Study points out that "Overall, religion is still at the cutting edge of philanthropy. Nearly three out of four people interviewed made a contribution to a church, synagogue, or religious charity during the year." And, the vast majority of adults say religion is "very important" to them or term it "fairly important."

Who is going to church?

■ **Women more so than men.** (This is good news because women outlive men, suggesting that religious donors can be counted on for longer periods of time!) It also bodes well for planned gifts. Will seminars and financial planning education aimed at women should increase their use of trusts and annuities.

■ **The more affluent:** by income and occupation, the rates are highest in the middle class and white-collar workers. By education, it tends to be college graduates. (As incomes go up, religious attendees also increase their giving to non-religious charities).

■ **Younger individuals seeking safer ways to socialization:** Churches are benefiting as Boomers and Busters' primary point of socialization moves into places of work, shopping, recreation, and worship.

The Bad News

For many individuals, religion is now interpreted as "spirituality" rather than linked to church attendance. This may be bad news for formal religious organizations even as it benefits other charities.

Specifically, in terms of religion, here are some concerns:

■ **The churchgoing population appears to be aging.** While people over 65 years of age are among the most generous givers by percentage of income (and give most of their contributions to religious charities), many make modest gifts. And, as younger adults increasingly understand their growing longevity, many are making smaller contributions to religious groups.

■ **Many Boomers are non-churchgoers.** Many religious organizations have not reattracted the younger adults who drifted away from religion in the '60s and '70s. Many of the mainstream churches are being hurt by past success. They are living off income earned from old wealth and feel no urgency to attract new supporters. Rather than reaching out and evangelizing, they expect people to come of their own accord.

■ **Churchgoing has declined among people in both executive, professional jobs and blue-collar workers.** The least likely to attend? Besides the young—blue-collar, and men, singles under 45, those with a low level of education, people in big cities and their suburbs and the poor.

■ **The amount members gave to their churches as a percentage of disposable income has dropped fairly steadily in just over two decades.** The decline is blamed in large part on the lack of fund-raising training given to pastors and other church leaders.

■ **A minority of church members now give a majority of funds.** Although typical in other charities, the move away from tithing and stewardship is a new situation for religion. Mission work has been hurt the most. One explanation is that with greater numbers of women in the workforce, fewer are actively participating in mission support.

■ **Boomers and Busters have explicit expectations for their churches.** They expect a high-quality kitchen, big meeting rooms, ample parking, child care, and clean bathrooms. They also want more space per person than their parents had. Younger adults look for high-quality preaching, music and social groups while their older counterparts are concerned with finding high-quality Sunday schools for their children.

■ **Younger individuals are more likely to have their first contact with a church at a weekday social function while older members**

typically are introduced on Sunday. Churches need to market themselves in terms of their functions: sites of weekday nursery schools, adult day care, aerobic dance groups, programs for latchkey kids, Alcoholics Anonymous meetings, adult literacy programs, and get togethers by numerous groups meeting for breakfast, lunch, dinner, and snacks.

Non-Religious Giving: New Priorities

Not every area charitable organization will fare equally well in fund raising in the upcoming years. Some are "hot" and some are not.

■ With government support declining, organizations representing the arts, health, and education have entered the fund raising arena. While support remains small from traditional audiences, a growing number of younger donors acknowledge the realities of life "after the welfare state" years.

■ Conservation/environment, international affairs, and youth have remained stable. They have attracted new audiences as well to replace declines in their traditional support. However, among them, only international affairs shows an increase.

■ Where is the growth? Younger audiences are supporting organizations specializing in science/technology, human services and public and societal benefit.

Recommendations for Increasing Support

■ **Arts/culture:** The interrelationship between those who attend arts events and those who support arts organizations through charitable giving is an especially close one. Few donors do not also hold subscriptions, memberships, or prove to be "return" attendees.

Currently, the majority of individual arts donors—especially to "traditional" arts organizations—are mature persons. Be sure to

Most Popular Charitable Beneficiaries

Percentage of the population giving to each category of charity

	BRITAIN	CANADA	FRANCE	SPAIN	USA
Social welfare*	14	11	2	39	8
Religion	16	29	6	22	33
Medicine & health	23	29	11	6	7
Civic & social**	5	10	4	3	7
Youth development	5	10	1	2	9
Education, training & employment	8	7	1	2	7
Arts, culture & humanities	2	5	1	1	2
Animals & wildlife	7	4	1	2	1
International aid	13	3	2	1	1

*Includes housing, elderly and human services
**Includes community action and human rights

SOURCE: Charities Aid Foundation, United Kingdom.

strengthen your ties with these donors. Often donors are not aware of how fragile the financial base of their favorite arts organizations is.

1. Communicate openly to your current supporters and back up the information with demonstrations of appreciation. Many arts donors respond well to plaques, certificates, special club membership and events.

2. Entice mature individuals by scheduling events at times and locations that appeal to them. Remember, many don't like driving at night. Print your brochures and invitations in larger type, using photographs of audience participants that demonstrate your appeal to the mature market.

3. Remember that, increasingly, the oldest in our societies are women—often widowed, divorced or single. Arts and cultural organizations offer unattached individuals an opportunity to participate via opening nights, preview exhibits, and VIP viewings in glittering special events where the lack of a partner is not a problem.

4. Think multigenerationally! As people live longer, many families by the year 2000 will include four generations. Consider marketing campaigns to attract grandparents, parents, and children as a group. In fact, older individuals like to mix with everybody. Cultural gatherings offer excellent opportunities for mature individuals to meet new people and make new friends.

Emphasize the networking opportunities for Boomers. "It's entertaining, and it's good for business," notes Mimi Johnson, vice president of Stephen Dunn & Associates, a fund-raising consulting firm specializing in telephone campaigns for arts organizations in the U.S. "Spending an evening at the opera, symphony, or ballet can make a good impression on the business contact you might bump into in the lobby."

1. Often, arts and cultural organizations appear unfriendly to younger prospects. Boomers need messages that they will be treated as special. Encourage them to join the leadership societies and accept their commitment with a quarterly or monthly pledge.

2. Arts organizations lend themselves to innovative special events. The glamour, the opportunity to dress up, and upscale ticket prices all

reinforce the Boomer's sense of being unique. Be sure to follow the cardinal rule if you want to attract this audience: keep them moving. Remember, Boomers attend your events for both business and social reasons. They can't mix freely if your event requires them to stay in place, at one table or without conversation, all the time.

Work the corporate connection. Support from the arts has often come from business—both from the contributions pocket and, increasingly, from the marketing budget.

1. Arts organizations must build a strong case for the arts' essential contribution to the individual and the community. Statistically and by example, demonstrate that the arts enhance an individual's self-esteem and skills and make the community a more attractive place to work.

2. Research has shown that purchasers base their buying decisions less on how products differ from each other than on how consumers view the companies that produce the products. Sponsorship polishes the image of a corporation. Demonstrate how support of your organization can either reach the traditional audiences or help to attract new individuals.

With the majority of college and university alumni coming from Boomers, educational institutions should be concerned. The loyalty of these alumni is not automatic. The college experience was not necessarily the one Boomers expected. Few colleges could resist the lure of increased admissions. The sudden expansion of college-age prospects resulted in packed lecture halls. As class sizes increased, intimacy decreased and, generally, weakened the emotional and loyalty ties educational fund raisers count so heavily upon.

Keys for reaching Boomer alumns include:

1. Provide them with positive information about their schools in a format they will accept. Statistics and anecdotes about the achievements of peer alumni can go a long way to rebuilding pride in their institutions. Include nostalgic pieces about their college experiences, respositioning the "negatives" into fond reminiscences.

2. Let Boomer alumni know the university welcomes their input. Boomers have a need to feel they have a continuing, respected role to

play in their alma maters. Invite them to take part in planning, to attend faculty senate meetings, student convocations, and other activities.

3. Encourage volunteerism. Boomers should be heavily represented on your board(s) and key committees. Give them significant roles to play. Always acknowledge their contributions of time and talent.

4. Sponsor networking activities where alumni can mix. Promote membership in leadership societies and giving clubs for their networking opportunities. Use "umbrella" reunions for all five-year milestones. Group alumni by area of interest rather than class. Hold events at convenient times and locations. Provide child care.

Women will be the majority of alumns in the future. The greatest challenge for colleges and universities may well be to demonstrate to women that their input and contributions are truly welcome. Keys for reaching women include, but are not limited to, adopting long-range cultivation strategies, aiming specific prospecting strategies to women, being more sensitive to women's concerns, recognizing differing demographics and psychographics among age groups, and understanding motivations.

■ **Health:** With health care costs spiraling, it's more and more difficult to convince younger prospects that hospitals and health care should be a charitable priority. Rather than focus on the community as a whole, increase your efforts to reach patients—current and former—and their families who have an emotional tie to your organization, which paves the way for gift giving.

Boomers represent the health-care decision-makers of the future. They are oriented towards wellness. Prevention and education are considered as important as treatment and cure. "Participatory" rather than "good" patients (the profile of mature individuals) they expect to be treated as equals in their medical experiences. Because Boomers tend to marry later, they are having children in their mid-30s, late 30s, and through their 40s. Boomer parents-to-be are an especially enticing audience for health-related development activities because they view everything about their birthing experiences as unique and will respond favorably to hospitals who reach out to them as partners.

Cultivation is the key. From the time that the expectant parent(s) choose a hospital, the institution must respond by making the Boomer(s) part of the "family." Childbirth classes should include the opportunity for an expectant parent(s)'s networking. Once the happy event occurs, the mother should be presented with a memento of the happy occasion. I especially like matching parent/child T-shirts with an appropriate message such as "ABC Hospital takes good care of me."

Steps in setting up a "Birth Fund"

1. Create a special program which suggests the establishment of a special fund to which family and friends can contribute—first, in honor of the birth, and in subsequent years, to note milestones such as "first teeth," "first steps," birthdays and achievements.

2. Create a brochure which suggests that making a gift to the hospital is a lasting way of expressing love for a new child and offer various examples (in a number of differing price ranges of needs such as purchasing equipment for the nursery or funding programs or services on the obstretics or pediatric ward.

3. Make it clear that gifts can be paid for over time through pledges and that contributions from many sources can be funnelled to the fund.

4. Offer to hold a celebration at the hospital once the initial fund goal is reached. All contributors have the opportunity to see their generosity in action, paving the way for future gifts.

The positive emotional environment that Boomer parents, along with other relatives and friends, enjoy will increase their receptiveness to making a special gift in honor of the forthcoming birth. Cultivation of those who have not used the hospital occurs as love for the new child links a network of friends and family to the health facility.

■ **Conservation/environment:** The environmental movement has changed dramatically in the space of about a decade. Public concerns about the environment rose to crisis proportions at the end of the 1980s. However, in the 1990s, concern declined. Partly this reflects a shift in focus to other pressing issues, but also the lowering of concern is caused by a perception that actions are being taken by government, businesses, and people themselves.

Concentrate on the most environmentally active segments of the population. All ages support environmental organizations. According to Roper Worldwide, the most environmentally active segments are the "True Blue Greens" and "Greenback Greens." True Blues are characterized by extremely high rates of activism in the form of recycling, donations to environmental groups, and avoidance of environmentally harmful products. Greenback Greens, meanwhile, show a remarkable willingness to pay higher prices for green products. Another segment, the "Sprouts," is a swing group with a middling level of "green" behavior and interest in the environment who have been shown to become more environmentally active with time.

Encourage social responsibility partnerships with corporations. The Body Shop, a British soap and lotion outfit that says it is "driven by values rather than profit" and works to "support human rights and cultural integrity of indigenous people," has demonstrated that concern breeds success. Revenues, profits, and store openings have all been impressively steady through recent rocky economic times.

Target Busters and Boomlets, who put the environment first on their list of priorities.

1. "Consumers no longer want to be thought of as consumers," notes Susan Hayward, director of the Yankelovich Monitor, a highly respected annual comprehensive consumer study. Young people are not as easy to reach through traditional media. There is a backlash against traditional advertising. Apple Computer provides free hardware to environmental groups. The partnership implies an endorsement.

2. Use music videos and movies as opposed to books and newspapers. The Audubon Society uses television specials to get viewers involved. As part of a special "If Dolphins Could Talk" about the

mammals' plight with pollution and tuna fishermen narrated by actor Michael Douglas, callers were able to access a toll-free "dolphin hot line." Callers were able to order a free activist kit and send protest messages to the tuna industry via a Western Union mailgram for a small fee. Western Union said the volume of calls it received in the two hours following the show was one of the highest in the company's history.

■ **International affairs:** younger generations have grown up in a world without boundaries. Because children tend to drive the philanthropy of their parents in affluent households, appeals in this area should continue to flourish.

Suggest gifts made in honor of Boomlets. Birthdays are an outstanding time to send appeals. Many affluent Boomlet children are so secure they gladly give away gift monies knowing that toys are always forthcoming from doting parents and grandparents.

For Busters, link volunteer service with philanthropy. Many young adults travel either during or immediately following college. Hands-on opportunities while abroad to see your program in action—and participate—will go far with this pragmatic audience.

■ **Youth:** as the baby Boomlet—a new generation of Civics—moves through childhood and the early teen years, youth organizations are likely to benefit. These children—unlike the Buster and Boomer generations—*like* being part of membership groups.

However, the composition of youth is changing. Increasingly the young of our societies will be more diverse—often the children of first generation immigrants or from minority populations. Not-for-profits will need to adapt to a rainbow coalition of parents who are proud of their ancestry but anxious to see their children succeed in mainstream society.

What these parents need from youth-focused organizations is similar to what previous generations wanted: after-school daycare, self-reliance courses, camping and weekend activities, as well as the counseling and health services that help young people grow up to be productive citizens.

But, unlike "traditional" parents, the parents of the Boomlet and beyond may need more information about what your organization is and reassurance that they are welcome. Use endorsements from the local community, provide materials in a variety of appropriate languages, use inclusive photographs, and be sensitive to customs and taboos.

Boomlet Values

Racial Harmony

73% have friends of another race

63% welcome someone of another race as a next-door neighbor

61% want to go to school with someone from another country

Charitable Giving

61% would give up some of their pocket money to help feed kids in poverty-stricken countries

50%+ would go without some presents at Christmas

37% would give up money for summer vacations

SOURCE: Louis Harris survey, 1992.

■ **Human services/public and societal benefit organizations:** as we shift from a Civic-dominated to an Idealistic-dominated prospect base, human service organizations, along with those who serve the community and society as a whole, will benefit. More and more philanthropic dollars are flowing to programs which support the needs of the elderly; counsel young people who abuse drugs, become pregnant, or drop out of school; offer solutions for social problems such as homelessness, child abuse, and domestic violence; and focus on a better community.

Position your marketing strategies heavily towards Boomers and Busters, especially women. They respond favorably to appeals which stress helping individuals over helping the system. Combine invitations for volunteerism with requests for contributions. Use case studies and real life examples, demonstrating how one individual was helped. Recruit Boomer and Buster "celebrity" help. Many younger entertainers are ready and willing to endorse your causes.

Don't forget that Boomers are increasingly a "sandwiched" generation. Many, especially Boomer women, are balancing health concerns for themselves and their families with emerging care needs of parents. Boomers are receptive to health and human service organizations that offer information and support services to the elderly and their families. Many Boomers are not overly concerned with inheriting the assets of their parents. They would prefer to know those assets are being put to use, assuring their parents of a comfortable older age. Use of planned giving/life income programs may be welcome if focused on providing dignity in the final years.

■ **Science/technology:** this may be a new twist on giving to education. It will appeal most heavily to Busters who are fascinated by technology. In fact, a Buster slogan is "The one who dies with the most toys wins!" Because Busters tend to be pragmatists, they'll expect you to show "win-win" situations for them. Demonstrate how their gifts are leveraged via challenge grants and strong stewardship.

Conclusion: Ethical Concerns for the Future

As fund raisers explore how to use demographic and psychographic tools most effectively, they also need to question how to use these powerful vehicles most ethically. Three key areas of potential abuse stand out:

- Who owns the information?
- Who owns the gift?
- Who owns the donor?

Who Owns the Information?

Not-for-profits are becoming increasingly sophisticated in research prospects and donors. Whether handled internally or externally, the amount of information being compiled is staggering.

The Issue of Confidentiality

Fund raisers must be aware that sensitive information carries responsibilities beyound legal liability. You must decide where to draw the line.

What's on the public record is astounding. Prospect research firms routinely provide information that goes well beyond stock holdings and transactions, business affiliations, and personal wealth. It regularly includes a prospect's giving interests, gift range, financial capacity, professional status and interests, social and business affiliations, and personal and family history. Collecting, and then dispersing information, can get sensitive: local newspapers often cover court cases involving messy divorces, criminal acts, and business improprieties which also become part of the prospect's record.

Credit reporting firms such as TRW in the U.S. have begun marketing to not-for-profits, mixing public domain information such as birth records and driver's licenses with private financial records. TRW's Performance Data System, for example, analyzes a charity's direct-mail files, as well as information in the corporation's own database, to determine the qualities that would make an individual most likely to respond to that charity's appeals. Then TRW provides a list, drawn from its files, of the names of people it judges most likely to contribute to the charity. Eventually, TRW expects to be able to rank the charity's donors as more or less likely to become major givers.

"You're really snooping when you use something like that," said John Gliha, director of prospect and systems services at the Iowa State University Foundation and past president of the American Prospect Research Association. "The information I use is really public information, and I don't consider that sort of information public."

Publicly available or privately collected, prospect information is extremely sensitive. Organizations need to have guidelines, follow them carefully, and maintain strict security measures to keep the reports from falling into unauthorized hands. Confidentiality is an important consideration.

Access to Information: A Donor's Right?

What about the rights of the donor or prospect to know that he or she is the subject of a file?

Thomas W. O'Connor, director of development at York College in Pennsylvania, objects to the practice of keeping such information without informing the subject of the research. "If something is being hidden from the prospective donor," he says, "then there's a problem right away. You measure it against yourself. How would you feel if someone were digging around in your own financial records?"

Steven E. Aufrecht, a privacy expert at the University of Alaska at Anchorage's School of Public Affairs, goes further. "People should know a file is being kept on them. And they should have some access to the files," says Aufrech, who has worked with the Puget Sound Prospect Research Association to define areas of ethical concern in fund raising. Researchers are divided over their responsibilites.

The question: a large donor to your institution calls and asks to review the file you have created on him. What do you respond?

58% Show him all the contents of the file.

24% Show him only part of his file, allowing him to believe that it is the entire file.

13% Show him part of his file and explain that there are materials in his file available only to development staff.

5% Refuse to show him the file at all.

SOURCE: American Prospect Research Association, 1989.

Who Owns the Gift?

Better Accountability and Stewardship

Royster C. Hedgepeth, senior vice president for development at the University of Colorado Foundation, notes that donors are often the last thought, if not an afterthought, when discussions of fund raising occur. Any discussion of funding must be based on donors' two basic rights:

- The right to expect that solicitations are made in the context of institutionally defined priorities.
- The right to expect that gifts will be used as the donor intended.

My own experiences, and those of other chief fund raisers, suggest that our donors do not believe they are getting accurate information from the institutions that solicit them. Increasingly, charities find gifts of smaller and smaller amounts being restricted as donors take stewardship and accountability into their own hands. This creates a funding dilemma for organizations who rely on unrestricted monies for operating expenses and to "seed" the fund-raising programs they conduct.

> **The demographics and psychographics of our emerging population groups suggest that, more than ever before, our donors and prospective donors will expect charities to *volunteer* detailed information on how their gifts will be used, and if any portion is earmarked for the costs of fund raising, explain how and why this is being done.**

Boomers—those who never trusted anyone over 30—increasingly dominate our donor and prospect lists. Organizations must respond forthrightly to their audiences' insistence on being given more and better information. More than any other cohort, Boomers are cynical about authority. Peter Dobkin Hall, himself a Boomer (b. 1946) and a consultant to historical and cultural organizations, asserts that

> The nonprofit sector as we know it is largely the creation of this generation—perhaps as many as two-thirds of the nonprofits now in existence came into being within the last 20 years. That these organizations were created at a time when the regulatory and funding environments were notably inhospitable to entities organized on a nonprofit basis is a tribute to the courage and civic-mindedness of 'those born after 1947.'

This, in turn, says Hall, combined with the turbulent circumstances and budgetary austerity of the 1970s and '80s, accounts for Boomers viewing themselves as "watchdogs for accountability."

Unless we communicate to donors and prospects—fully, honestly and openly—we will lose credibility with a constituency which values this above all else.

Unfortunately, few donors—Boomers or not—are happy knowing their gifts are being used for heat, light, and basic salaries. Donors expect their gifts to make an institution a better place. While most donors are not opposed to the use of some modest percentage of their gift to support fund-raising costs, notes Hedgepeth, donors respond positively when "the institutions using a portion of gifts in this manner emphasize the need to inform donors before the fact. Donors must be kept informed because they have the additional right to know they are making their investment in an organization that is cost-effective."

Because stewardship and accountability are key concerns of your donors and prospects, you need to provide them with information on how you address these issues *before* they make their gifts. Among the questions that need to be addressed:

■ **Who can accept gifts?** Does the fund raiser have that right? The chair of the trustees? Does gift acceptance require a full board/committee meeting? Gift acceptance policies will protect your organization: too often, before checking, a well-meaning volunteer tells the donor that his or her gift will be welcome. Sometimes gifts have complications. A policy that requires review by a committee provides a "cooling off" period.

■ **What types of gifts will your organization accept?** There may be a limit to what you want to handle in terms of management and stewardship. Your organization may not want any gifts of real estate or may want to accept such gifts only with the condition that such gifts of stock, and property are put up for sale immediately. You must balance out your ability to manage long-term assets with the potential donor's needs.

■ **How will you show your appreciation?** Recognition needs to be consistent for all donors. Decide levels for namings, endowments, and other types of fund raising. Will donors receive plaques or premiums? There's a cost involved. How much is to be given back?

■ **At what level may donors restrict their gifts?** As we go further up the gift-giving ladder, the proportion of gifts that come in with restrictions increases. Very few donors of one million dollars allow an organization to use their gift in any way the charity chooses. Where will you put the "breaks"?

■ **How will you recover operating and fund-raising costs from unrestricted, restricted and endowment gifts?** There are numerous methods for recovering fund-raising costs, ranging from levying a percentage tax on all restricted gifts to using unrestricted gifts to cover costs on restricted fund raising. Once you decide on your policy, volunteers and staff must communicate this information to potential donors.

■ **What levels of funding are required for endowments, scholarships, facility and room namings?** It needs to be consistent for all donors: you can't "sell" the same type of room to a member of the board for less than to the general public. And it's important not to accept less than is needed to handle the costs involved with the endowment's payout. It's better for everyone if the rules are set out clearly, in advance.

■ **How will you handle the possibility of immediate costs involved with an endowment gift?** For example, a donor who gives you a gift of stock. Your financial committee decides not to sell the stock, believing its value will increase substantially over the next few years. But the donor specifies that his gift fund an annual scholarship grant beginning immediately. How will you fund this?

■ **What about in-kind donations?** Do you take all that are offered? How are they valued (internally) to the organization?

In addition you should decide on your policy for sponsorship and cause-related marketing; your investment policies; use of paid versus commission-based fund-raising consultants; privacy of donor information issues; and of pledges and planned gifts.

Once you've formulated the initial answers to these questions, create a document titled "Gift Stewardship Guidelines and Policies" and make it available to all concerned. You should also consider adding a line onto all your fund-raising materials indicating that you have a written policy in place and offer to provide your guidelines brochure upon request.

Your gift stewardship guidelines will expand as your fund-raising efforts grow. It is a living document that needs to be updated yearly by board and staff to reflect the maturing of your development program. Sample guidelines are found at the end of this chapter.

Who Owns the Donor?

Look around any professional meeting of fund raisers . . . half are new to their jobs and the other half are looking!

Boomers: A Restless Generation

Fund raisers mirror the population as a whole. Like the rest of our populations, fund raisers are increasingly Boomers. And, job wise, Boomers are more mobile than previous generations. Landon Jones, author of *Great Expectations*, attributes this, in part, to the fierce competition for top positions. "In effect, the entire generation will be like a large group of people being moved from a big room into a smaller room." Those Boomers who find advancement blocked at one organization may opt to move on.

"People are less wedded to the institution of a career," says Harvard Professor Robert Reich, himself a Boomer. "Almost all of my friends are doing different things from five years ago, and five years ago, they were doing different things from five years before. Success today is more a subjective condition based in your own head than an objective condition established by society."

During the 1970s and '80s, the constituencies of many not-for-profits expanded dramatically. Colleges and universities, the most visible example, found their alumni populations doubling, even tripling, in a matter of years, because of the influx of Boomers as students. Fund-raising offices expanded staff to keep pace. Today, the new professionals who joined the fund-raising staffs of many charities a decade or more ago are seasoned veterans. Like all Boomers, they continue to seek resources and recognition. They want to be "appeals directors," "heads of fund raising," or another title that acknowledges their expertise and compensates them well. The high rate of turnover we see is, often, a realistic reaction to fund raisers' appraisals of opportunities for promotion within a not-for-profit.

Sustaining Donor/Institution Relationships

Especially in major gift fund raising, relationships are forged over time. The cycle of cultivation to solicitation may take months or years to develop. Successful major gift fund raising is dependent on the prospect having confidence and trust in the individual who represents the organization.

If you changed jobs, how much of the prospect information would you take to your new institution?

12% would take all the information

30% would take none

58% would take some

SOURCE: American Prospect Research Association, 1989.

While most organizations say they prefer to have major gift cultivation done by volunteers with the professional fund raiser "off stage," big gift prospects are increasingly being handled by the fund-raising staff. As a result, it is not uncommon for a close relationship to form between donor and fund raiser.

The mobility of fund raisers brings up potential concerns. Will the donor transfer loyalty to a new organization? Will the development officer, in fact, encourage this practice? What must the fund raiser say when asked by the donor about the new agency he or she now represents? What if no gift has yet been received from the prospect, and he or she may, in fact, not be a good match for the first organization, but might possibly be sincerely interested in the fund raiser's new charity?

These concerns are not new. However, the quickening tempo of job changes makes guidelines more important than ever to avoid charges of unethical behavior.

Conclusion

I began this book by noting that demographics and psychographics are powerful. There is little question that fund raisers have entered exciting times, with the opportunity to use newly available tools on behalf of deserving organizations.

Even fund raisers wet their fingers and rub signatures on letters. Today's technology often makes it difficult to identify "the real thing." Add increasingly sophisticated use of file material to create letters which suggest to a prospect or donor that he or she is being addressed personally; include phrases and examples that key into that person's identified demographics and psychographics; and send it out in a machine-calligraphied envelope with what appears to be a first-class stamp—when does a development strategy overstep the parameters and cease being ethical?

It's not a question of how far can we go but, rather, how far *should* we go. Each organization should be alert to possible abuses and develop guidelines, in advance of using these powerful tools, to cover possible abusive situations.

Bill Olcott, editor of *Fund Raising Management* magazine, may have summed it up best in an editorial he wrote entitled "Winning and Ethics":

> You hear a lot these days about winning. Everybody loves a winner; losers are looked down on. But this drive to win, while good in itself, can go out of control to become winning at all costs...Fund raisers are held to a higher ethical standard. It's great to win, but it's not always possible. The runners-up are not losers; competing at a high level is what counts. A lot of our ethical problems would be solved if we approached them with this attitude.

As we move through the remainder of the 1990s and approach the 21st century, let's use our new demographic and psychographic tools to help our organizations better fulfill their missions. But, let us also remember our primary obligation: to do so ethically.

Sample Gift Stewardship and Accountability Guidelines*

1. What types of gifts does ABC organization accept?

The ABC Organization accepts gifts of cash, securities, irrevocable planned-gift arrangements utilizing bequests, life insurance, trusts and annuities, as well as in-kind and real-property contributions.

- Stock gifts are attributed the median price on the day received.
- Gifts of real property valued at $5,000 and over should be evaluated by an independent appraiser. The ABC Organization does not assign a value for tax purposes to non-cash contributions, although it will assign a general "internal" level for donor recognition.
- Pledges paid within a five-year period are assigned full, current value. Until they are "paid in full," they are considered to be "accounts receivable" and assigned 70% of value.
- Deferred gifts (including, but not limited to, annuities, unitrusts, pooled-income vehicles, and irrevocable bequests) are assigned a value, adjusted for current value using actuarial tables for the age of the donor.
- Bequests that are revocable are assigned a value of $1,000. If the actual amount is known it is recorded for an "internal" level of donor recognition only.

2. Who can accept gifts on behalf of ABC?

An outright, unrestricted cash gift of any amount may be accepted by the executive director, development staff, or members of the board.

---

*This document was developed for the legal requirements of the United States. It may be useful for you to discuss your country's requirements with your trustees and staff as you develop your own guidelines.

A non-cash gift (including real property, stock, or a planned-gift vehicle) or restricted cash gifts (allowed at $1,000 or greater) may be accepted by the executive director, development staff, or members of the board subject to a review by ABC Organization's finance committee. The review will be scheduled within a 45-day period.

3. What forms of donor recognition are given?

All gifts to the ABC Organization are sincerely appreciated and promptly acknowledged with a letter.

Unless a donor requests anonymity, all contributors for the immediate past fiscal year (July 1–June 30) are listed in an Annual Report/Honor Roll of Donors.

Donors who contribute at and above $100 are considered to be members of ABC's Patron's Circle:

Members	$100 to $999 annual gifts
Contributors	$1,000 to $9,999 annual gifts
Benefactors	$10,000 and above cumulative gifts
Key Club	Bequests and planned gifts

A personalized certificate of appreciation is provided to members of the Patron's Circle upon request.

For membership in the Key Club, donors must indicate, in writing, that they have included the ABC Organization or a particular department in their wills or other planned-giving vehicle. No amount need be specified.

4. How are fund-raising costs recovered from contributions?

The ABC Organization raises funds on behalf of the organization and its entities through an intensified development strategy utilizing personal solicitations, corporate and foundation proposals, direct mail, telecommunications, and special events.

- All direct costs for fund raising are recovered from these efforts before funds are distributed.
- 20% of each undesignated gift is assigned to the Office of Development to cover the costs of fund raising.
- For designated or restricted gifts, direct costs of fund raising are recovered by the following formula:

10% levy for gifts of up to $100,000

5% levy for gifts of over $100,000

This levy can be "paid" in any of the following ways:

- with donor agreement, taken from the gift
- with donor agreement, supplementing the gift
- with department agreement, taken from another source of revenue including unrestricted and designated funds

- After fund-raising costs are recovered, the ABC Organization will then allocate the remaining unrestricted dollars among its entities and departments. Recommendations for distribution will be made quarterly by the administrators' council.

5. What levels of funding are required for a named endowment?

$10,000 or greater establishes a named endowment fund. The first grant is made during July following completion of the first full fiscal year after the fund's establishment. The grant is limited to 5% from the interest income, with the remaining interest going back into the endowment to build principal.

6. What levels of funding are required for trusts and annuities?

$50,000 establishes a charitable remainder trust or annuity. Generally, these are made available to individuals age 55 or over. Up to two beneficiaries may be incorporated to receive payments. The funding of the trust or annuity must be done with a vehicle which can be readily liquidated prior to payments commencing.

7. What are the requirements for bequest gifts?

Bequest gifts of any amount are welcome. Because it is difficult to anticipate the needs of the future, donors are requested to leave their bequest gifts to ABC Organization unrestricted, or designated rather than restricted.

8. What kinds of in-kind donations are accepted?

A limited amount of office equipment, durable goods, and specific materials in good condition is needed. In-kind gifts are assigned no value by the ABC Organization. It is the responsibility of the donor to do so for tax purposes.

9. What is ABC Organization's policy for sponsorship and cause-related marketing? For premiums and incentives?

ABC Organization recognizes that its name carries weight in our community. Before agreeing to lend its implied endorsement to a for-profit entity through sponsorship and/or cause-related marketing, the sponsorship committee will meet, review the request, and advise the board. A decision will be rendered within 45 days of the request.

Fund-raising appeals which, in exchange for a contribution, offer premiums or incentives (the value of which is not insubstantial, but which is significant in relation to the amount of the donation) will advise the donor of the fair market value of the premium or incentive and that the value is not deductible for tax purposes.

10. What are ABC Organization's investment policies?

As an ethical, responsible member of our community, ABC Organization will not invest in stock/bond vehicles that either directly or indirectly refute our mission. These include: tobacco, drug and alcohol products, as well as companies with a history of discriminating by race/ethnicity, age, gender, or sexual orientation. We do not do business with countries that ignore the civil rights of their citizens.

11. What is ABC Organization's stance on the use of paid versus commission-based fund-raising consultants?

ABC subscribes to the principles of both the American Association of Fund-Raising Counsel and the National Society of Fund Raising Executives. We do not hire fund raisers on a percentage basis.

12. What is ABC Organization's stance on privacy of donor information issues?

ABC recognizes that donors are at the heart of our organization's viability and that we have a strong responsibility to protect their privacy.

- All donors are contacted prior to the printing of the annual Honor Roll in the September issue of our newsletter and advised that names are being listed. Donors are given the option of remaining anonymous.
- Donors are welcome to request and receive a complete copy of any written materials being held in their file.
- Only authorized staff and board members may view a donor file.
- Donor files remain on-site.

SOURCE: expanded from *Targeted Fund Raising: Defining and Refining Your Development Strategy*, Judith E. Nichols, Precept Press 1991.

Bibliography

I drew upon a variety of resources in my research. Here is a sampling of those publications and organizations I found especially helpful.

The Affluence Index, 1992-93 Edition
Concert Music Network 1992

Agewave
Ken Dychtwald with Joe Flower
Tarcher 1988

The Barna Report, 1992-93
George Barna
Regal Books 1992

Beyond Mind Games: The Marketing Power of Psychographics
Rebecca Piirto
American Demographics Books 1991

Capturing Customers: How to Target the Hottest Markets of the '90s
Peter Francese and Rebecca Piirto
American Demographics Books 1991

Future Tense: The Business Realities of the Next Ten Years
Ian Morrison and Greg Schmid
William Morrow & Company 1994

Genderflex: Men & Women Speaking Each Other's Language at Work
Judith C. Tingley, Ph.D.
AMACOM 1994

Generations: The History of America's Future, 1584 to 2069
William Strauss and Neil Howe
William Morrow & Company 1991

Great Expectations: America and the Baby Boom Generation
Landon Y. Jones
Ballantine 1980

The Lifestyle Odyssey
Editors of *Research Alert*
Sourcebooks 1992

Marketing to Boomers and Beyond
David B. Wolfe
McGraw Hill 1993

Marketing to and through Kids
Selina S. Guber and Jon Berry
McGraw Hill 1993

Marketing to the Affluent, Selling to the Affluent, Networking with the Affluent
Dr. Thomas J. Stanley
Dow-Jones Irwin 1988

Market Ownership: The Art & Science of Becoming #1
William A. Sherden
AMACOM 1994

Market Segmentation: Using Demographics, Psychographics and Other Niche Marketing Techniques to Predict Customer Behavior
Art Weinstein
Probus 1994

The Master Trend: How the Baby Boom Generation is Remaking America
Cheryl Russell
Plenum Press 1993

Multicultural Marketing
Marlene L. Rossman
AMACOM 1994

The One to One Future: Building Relationships One Customer at a Time
Don Peppers and Martha Rogers, Ph.D.
Currency/Doubleday 1993

Relationship Fundraising
Ken Burnett
White Lion Press (UK) 1992

Reinventing Fundraising: Realizing the Potential of Women's Philanthropy
Sondra C. Shaw and Martha A. Taylor
Jossey-Bass 1995

The Seasons of Business: The Marketer's Guide to Consumer Behavior
Judith Waldrop with Marcia Mogelonsky
American Demographics Books 1992

Segmenting the Women's Market: Using Niche Marketing to Understand and Meet the Diverse Needs of Today's Most Dynamic Consumer Market
E. Janice Leeming and Cynthia F. Tripp
Probus 1994

Selling the Story: The Layman's Guide to Collecting and Communicating Demographic Information
William Dunn
American Demographics Books 1992

Targeting the New Professional Women
Gerry Myers
Probus 1994

Women and Philanthropy
Anne I. Thompson and Andrea R. Kaminski
University of Wisconsin-Madison Press 1993

Women as Donors, Women as Philanthropists
Abbie J. von Schlegell and Joan M. Fisher, Editors
New Directions for Philanthropic Fundraising, Number 2,
Jossey-Bass, Winter 1993

Sources for Demographic and Psychographic Information Directly Pertinent to Not-for-Profits

The Chronicle of Philanthropy
1255 23rd Street, NW
Washington, DC 20037
(202) 466-1200

Donors **Magazine** (devoted to the use and application of information technology in fund raising)
CVSS, Compton Martin
Bristol BS18 8JP
United Kingdom
For a free sample copy call
(44) 0761-221810 or Fax (44) 0761-221910

The Foundation Center (publishers of *The Foundation News*)
79 Fifth Avenue
New York, NY 10003
(800) 424-9836

Fund Raising Management **Magazine**
224 Seventh Street
Garden City, NY 11530
(516) 746-6700

Giving and Volunteering in the United States
Independent Sector
1828 L Street, NW, Suite 1200
Washington, DC 20036
(202) 223-8100

Giving USA
AAFRC Trust for Philanthropy
25 West 43rd Street
New York, NY 10036
(212) 354-5799

Individual Giving and Volunteering in Britain: Who gives what and why?
Conducted for Charities Aid Foundation, 1993
48 Pembury Road
Tonbridge, Kent TN9 2JD
United Kingdom

The Mind of the Donor
Barna Research Group, Ltd.
647 West Broadway
Glendale, CA 91204
(818) 241-9300

The Non-Profit Times
P.O. Box 408
Hopewell, NY 08525
(609) 466-4600

***Professional Fundraising* Magazine**
4 Market Place
Hertford, Herts SG14 1EB
Great Britian
44 01992 501177

Relationship Fundraising
Ken Burnett
White Lion Press (UK) 1992

About the Author

Judith E. Nichols, Ph.D., CFRE, is an Oregon-based development consultant with a variety of not-for-profit clients across the U.S. and in Canada and Europe. A popular trainer and presenter, she specializes in helping organizations understand the implications of our changing demographics and psychographics on fund raising, marketing, and membership. Dr. Nichols has been featured at numerous conferences, workshops, and symposia in the United States, Europe, and Canada.

Dr. Nichols is the editor of *Philanthropy Trends that Count*, a quarterly newsletter, and is a columnist for *Contributions*. She has been interviewed by many publications, including *The Chronicle of Philanthropy* and the *Irish Times*, and her articles have appeared in *Fund Raising Management, The Non-Profit Times* and *Professional Fund Raising*.

She has more than 20 years of fund raising and marketing experience, working with higher education as well as with arts and cultural, health-related, human benefit and social service, membership, and youth organizations. Clients include the American Heart Association, Girl Scouts of the USA, the Presbyterian Church (USA) Foundation, and the National Society for the Prevention of Cruelty to Children (UK).

An NSFRE-certified senior fund raiser, Dr. Nichols served as Vice President for Development at Portland State University, Oregon, and headed an award-winning development program at Wayne State University, Detroit, and at the New Jersey Institute of Technology.

Index

C

N

O

P

Q-R

Additional books by Dr. Nichols

Growing from Good to Great:
Positioning your fund-raising efforts for BIG gains **$40**

"A really great read! . . . Provides important insight and direction for community nonprofit organization managers and fund raisers from now on into the challenges of 2000 plus."

— Charles Stephens
Indiana University
Center on Philanthropy

Pinpointing Affluence:
Increasing Your Share of Major Donor Dollars **$40**

" . . . a highly informative book that can strengthen your fund-raising program by prompting you to rethink who your best donors are and redirect your efforts toward those capable and willing to give."

— *The Complete Professional's Library*

Targeted Fund Raising:
Defining and Refining Your Development Strategy **$40**

"Right on target . . . sound, practical advice on fund raising with a perceptive examination of the trends affecting individual, foundation, and corporate donors today. A lucid work, ***Targeted Fund Raising*** helps you separate the wheat from the chaff."

— *Contributions*

Changing Demographics:
Fund Raising in the 1990s **$40**

" . . . gives fund raisers a view of *their* destiny. Helps put the trends into a coherent perspective. It's a fascinating and enlightening review."

— *CASE Currents*

Judy Nichols' books are available from: